THE BRITISH EMPIRE
PART ONE

Plays by John Spurling

Macrune's Guevara
In the Heart of the British Museum
Shades of Heathcliff *and* Death of Captain Doughty

THE BRITISH EMPIRE PART ONE

a play by
JOHN SPURLING
with an introductory essay by the author

Marion Boyars
London Boston

Published in 1982 in Great Britain and the United States by
MARION BOYARS PUBLISHERS
18 Brewer Street, London W1R 4AS
and
99 Main Street, Salem, New Hampshire 03079

© John Spurling 1982

All performing rights in John Spurling's plays are strictly reserved and application for performances should be made to
MacNaughton Lowe Representation Limited
194 Old Brompton Road, London SW5 0AS, England

No performance of this play may be given unless a licence has been obtained prior to rehearsal.

All rights reserved.
No part of this publication may be reproduced, stored in a retrieval system or transmitted in any form, by any means, electronic, mechanical, photocopying, recording or otherwise except brief extracts for the purpose of review, without the prior permission of the publisher.
Any paperback edition of this book whether published simultaneously with, or subsequent to, the casebound edition is sold subject to the condition that it shall not, by way of trade, be lent, resold, hired out or otherwise disposed of without the publisher's consent, in any form of binding or cover other than that in which it was published.

Spurling, John
The British Empire, part one.
I. Title
822'.914   PR6069.P8

ISBN 0-7145-2743-2
ISBN 0-7145-2732-7 PbK
Library of Congress Catalog Card Number 81-52338

Printed and bound in Great Britain at
The Camelot Press Ltd, Southampton

"Ichabod, Ichabod,
The glory is departed!
Travels Waring East away?
Who, of knowledge, by hearsay,
Reports a man upstarted
Somewhere as a god,
Hordes grown European-hearted,
Millions of the wild made tame
On a sudden at his fame?
In Vishnu-land what Avatar?"

Robert Browning

"For he that once hath missed the right way,
The further he doth goe, the further he doth stray."

Edmund Spenser

"I hold that the real policy of England is to be the champion of justice and right: pursuing that course with moderation and prudence, not becoming the Quixote of the world, but giving the weight of her moral sanction and support wherever she thinks justice, and wherever she thinks that wrong has been done."

Lord Palmerston

"In order to rule over barbarians, you have got to become a barbarian yourself."

George Orwell

INTRODUCTION

No one expects historical accuracy from Shakespeare's history plays. Their content is partly contemporary; actions and ideas which entertained Elizabethans, and partly perennial; human nature. All the same they were based on history (especially Holinshed's version of it) and some of their force rested and still rests on the assumption that such and such actually happened (even if it didn't), that it shaped England and English society and that it is worth dramatizing as a moral precedent for living Englishmen.

In writing history plays today, we have to do rather better than Shakespeare on the score of accuracy. There are far more sources; infinitely more is known about the past and audiences are better informed. The playwright has to be, if not quite a historian, at least a student of history. He can claim a certain artistic licence, but not as much as if he were writing farce, romance, melodrama, satire, or whatever. There's no point in using real people and events from the past in order to construct something significant for the present (which I take to be the purpose of a serious history play) if you deliberately garble the facts. It may be good theatre – a tract in historical costume like *St. Joan*, for instance – but it doesn't have the extra weight of being a true story. Just because Shakespeare garbled the facts, even if unintentionally, accepting the Tudor Government line and giving it the charge of his own passion for order, legitimacy and reconciliation, doesn't entitle us to do the same in the late 20th century when we no longer live in a simple, one-party state.

Of course no story is objectively true. History – or at least its superstructure, in the Marxian analysis – is an interpretation, not a science. The truth lies in the playwright's intention. Did he set out to understand what happened or only to use it as a means to some predetermined end of his own? His prejudices and beliefs naturally colour his interpretation, but one should also feel a pull the other way, that the discovery of the facts has coloured his beliefs and prejudices. A history play, it goes almost without saying, is a political play, but not in the narrow sense that 'political theatre' has acquired during the seventies. 'Political theatre' is written by playwrights or directed by directors who have become 'politicized', that's to say converted to a simple-minded, missionary-style Marxism. Marx and Engels themselves, beavering away at their grand theory to explain the basic structure of history, took a rather less rigid view of its superstructure than many of their followers give them credit for. As it happens, their grand theory being what it was, they did in the long term approve of the British Empire, since they saw it as breaking up the old ('Asiatic') economies and setting them on the only possible road to an improved future, via capitalism; but in the short term they wholly disapproved of it and in this they were much too sweeping, unable to see from their enclosed, intellectual position at the centre of the Empire exactly what went on at the edges. It was not wrong to say, as Marx did in 'The Future Results of the British Rule in India', that in the Empire 'the profound hyopocrisy and inherent barbarism of bourgeois civilization lay unveiled, turning from its home where it assumed respectable forms, to the colonies, where it went naked', but it was a half-truth. I suppose that if I had been 'politicized' I should have been content with that half-truth and have arrived at a play which the many servants of fashion and orthodoxy in our theatre might have considered broadly 'correct'.

Actually I started from a state of confusion. Born and partly brought up in a British colony in Africa, educated at a notably tough Victorian public-school in England, living during the holidays with my grandmother (who was born the year before Gordon's death at Khartoum), commissioned as a National Serviceman in the Royal Artillery, I had acquired by the age of twenty most of the standard values and opinions associated with the British Empire. Which is not, of course, to say that there weren't other aspects to my character. At the age of eleven I had stopped wanting to be a sailor and decided, after seeing and reading Shakespeare and writing a play of my own, to be a playwright, a project which in my eyes even then was definitely a form of protest against rugger, cricket and all that lay behind them. I was not good at games and therefore not a successful schoolboy, never for instance a prefect. At Oxford my protest became more aggressive and the ruling hearties of my college even accorded me the aesthete's accolade of wrecking my room.

Nevertheless, reluctantly or not, I was trained and in many ways suited to take my place as a District Officer in some remote dependency and when I left Oxford in 1960 I was given a temporary job as a Plebiscite Officer in the then British Cameroons. I think the Colonial Office had their money's worth. I was a conscientious and rigorously impartial official. But, of course, though I approached my task in the good old empire-building, empire-maintaining way – even uncovering with Sleemanesque zeal a substantial voting fraud in one village – I was actually helping to pull the thing down. (The Cameroons, a UN Trust Territory, was being offered the choice of joining one or other of its recently independent neighbours, Nigeria or the Cameroun Republic.) I found too, as I'd previously found in the army, that I didn't really like being a prefect. Towards the end of my time in the Cameroons I began to assert my own independence in rather childish ways, taking a black girl to dinner in the white administrators' restaurant – an appallingly embarrassing experience for both of us, though not of course prohibited; getting hopelessly drunk on a beach and being saved from drowning only by the arrival of a party of UN Observers, and so on. It's hardly surprising that someone as deeply imbued as I was with imperial values should have become unsettled by their sudden redundancy. I wanted to believe that we were doing the best, the decent thing by shrugging off our responsibility for this tiny, unimportant strip of rain forest, but surrounded by the petty corruption of its politicians, the unreliability of my local assistants, the primitive poverty of the villages with their drunken men and beast-of-burden women, I could only feel that if we had no right to be there in the first place, we had even less to get out now. At the time there was a civil war going on in the Cameroon Republic; the British Cameronians chose to join them nonetheless and so avoided becoming involved a few years later in the Biafran war. But even to characterize them as British Cameronians is absurd. They were a welter of tribes speaking a welter of languages, whose territory had been first grabbed by the Germans and then, during the First War, by us.

After I'd returned from Africa and as the British Empire was finally dismantled, I became infected like so many others with disillusionment, distaste and contempt for the whole sordid imperial episode. The Empire had been a bad thing. The British had been better people and truer to themselves before they acquired vast possessions and ruled a quarter of the world's population; the White Man's Burden must be discarded as false and pernicious.

I was still in the grip of this slightly hysterical reaction when I began reading and making notes for my play in 1975. But I didn't have to do much research to realize that to be anti-imperialist was as foolish as to be imperialist. Foolish because irrelevant. The Empire, the rock-fast world I had thought I belonged to and grown up into, did not go back into the mists of time, it hardly even went back into the 19th century. It was a creation of the last years of Victoria's reign, the late Eighties and Nineties. Did that world go shopping at Harrods and Barkers? They had not existed earlier. Were all respectable British Imperial males circumsized? Only since 1891, when a certain Dr. Remondino took the middle-classes by storm with a book called *History of Circumcision* in which he urged that 'parents cannot make a better saving investment for their little boys, as it ensures them better health, greater capacity for labour, longer life, less nervousness, sickness, loss of time, and less doctor bills, as well as it increases their chances for an euthanasian death'.

These are somewhat trivial examples, yet the very word 'imperialism' in its modern sense only goes back a hundred years. Lord Carnarvon, Disraeli's Colonial Secretary, said in 1878: 'We have been of late much perplexed by a new word, "Imperialism", which has crept in amongst us'. The public-school ethos of manliness through sport, it's true, dates from a bit earlier – the 1860s, but the colony I was born in, and indeed most of the African colonies, were not acquired until the nineties. So the British Empire at its height lasted some sixty or seventy years, hardly longer than the Athenian Empire (that democratic joke and abortion), no comparison with Rome's monolith; and for most of that period it was already hollow inside since, from the First War on, the thing was less a power-structure (though Hitler for one was misled by the facade) than a crumbling edifice still held together by the pressure of its own weight. The basis of my childhood *Weltanshauung*, then, was no more than the last phase of the Empire, at once climax and dissolution. And another odd thing: the only considerable Imperial action of this climax – the Boer War – was neither glorious nor, in its results, successful. I began to see this supposedly wicked, powerful, patronising, authoritarian, self-confident, strutting Empire without any clothes, *castrato* as well as circumsized.

But if the Empire was such a poor thing in its palmiest days, at a time when the public actually knew about it and felt a sense of pride in it, perhaps its real power and glory had existed earlier, during the sixty-five years or so between the aftermath of Waterloo and the fall of Khartoum; the period when Marx was observing it from the shelter of the British Museum? Not so. It grew, certainly, but haphazardly and spasmodically. No one in the British Government – not Palmerston, not even Disraeli – wanted it to grow and many, such as James Stephen, Permanent Secretary of the Colonial Office at roughly mid-century, were actively opposed to its growing anywhere except in the 'empty' lands, Canada and Australia. The public in general hardly knew it was there and certainly didn't care. The people on the ground, soldiers, explorers, missionaries and traders created it almost unconsciously in the natural process of their professions and from a mixture of motives, good, bad and indifferent.

The conquest of India was started at the end of the 18th

century because French and British trading interests clashed and the French lost and were ousted. Local potentates inevitably made alliances against their rivals with the superior technologists on their doorstep and in due course both allies and opponents dwindled into a client position. The process of piecemeal acquisition lasted until 1856, the year before the Mutiny, when the most loyal ally of all, the King of Oudh, was removed from power because of the irredeemable corruption and inefficiency of his regime. A decade earlier the fierce Sikh Wars had broken out essentially because of a power vacuum after the death of the Punjab's outstanding and British-allied ruler, Ranjit Singh. In this case the Sikhs, with their European-trained, well-gunned and aggressive army, were the expansionists, although the outcome was the British annexation of the Punjab. The province of Sind had been seized in 1843 by the eccentric and irresistibly sympathetic General Charles Napier, because its ruling Amirs had become uppity after the British reverse in Afghanistan and because in any case they were bad rulers and detested by their subjects. That was of course no reason for seizing someone else's country, as Napier fully admitted, calling his own action 'a very advantageous, useful, humane piece of rascality', but Napier and his lieutenants, including the young Richard Burton, certainly did a great deal to make life more tolerable for the ordinary people of Sind. As for the Amirs, they had suffered injustice, but in Napier's opinion someone always did and 'on a crew more deserving to bear it, hardly could it alight'. I meant to have Napier in my play, but he really needs a play to himself.

So the conquest of India could only not have happened if Europeans had never gone to trade there in the first place and for that reason I have judged it outside the scope of this play. What the British did in India once they were established is of course another matter and this I have tried to test against our own consciences. One of the key points in the play is the decision to invade Afghanistan. Whether that was really the significant moment when the British Empire lost its innocence and acted unequivocally – like the US in Vietnam or the USSR again in Afghanistan – from a combination of fear, stupidity and immorality, I can't be sure, but I have chosen it as the moment and have placed the consequences not only as the direct military disaster which overtook the British army of occupation but also, by implication, the moral and political disaster of the Indian Mutiny sixteen years later. That in its turn led to the increasing separation of the British from their subject peoples as the century went on and so to many of the evils we associate with 'imperialism'; thus in the end to that sense of guilt and failure which overcame us in the 1950s and 60s as we withdrew from the Empire.

But if one looks afresh at that period of 'innocence', during the 1820s and 30s, it is clear that, outside India, the Empire owed as much to idealism as to imperialism. Blinded by the great dazzle of the end of the century, with its huge territorial expansion, its Queen Empress, its proconsuls and imperial viziers – Cromer, Rhodes, Salisbury, Chamberlain – we have tended to ignore the fact that Britain was, after all, a kind of democracy (even if on a severely limited suffrage) and that opinion was always divided. Gladstone was vociferously anti-imperialist, though a tangled knot of circumstances caused him to bombard Alexandria and occupy Egypt in the eighties, horrifying his Liberal supporters. In South Africa at the same time he was withdrawing, refusing to avenge the British defeat at Majuba Hill in the First Boer War. He withdrew too in Afghanistan and tried to give Home Rule to Ireland. One of the ironies of Gladstone's career is that he made his mark when he first entered Parliament in a maiden speech *against* the abolition of slavery (his father had grown rich from sugar estages in the West Indies), for Gladstone himself later became almost the embodiment of the tradition of liberal humanitarianism. I have been accused of leaving economics out of this play and I will come back to that. But a much more serious omission from a piece chiefly concerned with the moral questions raised by the Empire is the whole business of the slave-trade and its suppression.

I tried to get Wilberforce in (a scene with the still unregenerate young Gladstone) and I wrote a set of scenes covering Commander Denman's Nelsonic attack on the slavers of the Gallinas; they didn't work and anyway the play was already too long. But Wilberforce and the ideas associated with him and the Clapham Sect were quite as important to the nature of the Empire as Palmerston and his essentially European-orientated power politics. Palmerston himself, of course, was all for suppressing the slave trade, even though he had tenants on his Irish estates whose condition was little better than that of slaves. In 1845, when a Parliamentary Committee looked into the matter, no less than one fifth of the Royal Navy was employed off the West Coast of Africa stopping slavers and bringing them before the international courts set up under Britain's aegis in Freetown. The Committee assessed the cost to the British Government of fighting the slave-trade at £600,000 a year. There were many who thought it too expensive, but the humanitarians had their way and the campaign – hopeless as long as the US and Brazil continued to use slaves – went on until the North beat the South in the American Civil War.

The side-effects of this costly crusade ran right through the early 19th century Empire. Governor Arthur of Tasmania (he knew it as Van Diemen's Land) may have been a rather ridiculous martinet, but he was also (having taken part as a junior officer in the West Indies in the suppression of a slave rebellion) a dedicated convert to the ideas of the Clapham Sect. He helped bring about the extinction of the Tasmanian aborigines with the very best intentions. Gordon Laing, the discoverer of Timbuctoo, was a subaltern in Sierra Leone who caught the exploring bug during an expedition into the interior to examine the local effects of slaving. George Maclean engineered a treaty between the Ashantis and the Fantis and brought many years of peace to the strife-torn Gold Coast, which had been previously abandoned by the British as a useless and dangerous territory. Maclean had no official position except as an employee of the local British traders, yet he was roundly ticked off by Lord Glenelg, the Clapham-inspired Colonial Secretary, because one of the terms of his treaty was that the Fantis would return runaway slaves to the Ashantis. To keep Maclean in his place and make it clear that, whatever his good relations with the natives, he was not governing British territory, his rank was never raised above that of local Captain.

Natal and Zululand were other places the British Government didn't want at any price, yet the private energies of British subjects and the complication of circumstances again forced the Government, as happened later in the Gold Coast, to take responsibility in the end. The Boers set out on their Great Trek and occupied the interior of South Africa – one of the chief reasons for the eventual British annexation of Natal and Zululand, not to speak of Rhodesia at the end of the century – because they refused to live under a Government which had abolished slavery. General Gordon went to the Sudan in the first place to try to stop the slave-trade there. His death at Khartoum was partly due to the British Government refusing to replace him as Governor General with the notorious slaver Zubair Pasha, who would probably have had the power and standing to defeat the Mahdi. There were no slaves in India, but William Sleeman cleaned up the Thugs from the same irreproachably humane and altruistic motives as the anti-slavery people. His methods, it's true, were high-handed; otherwise he would have been no more successful than those who in this century have tried to clean up the Mafia. Other idealistic Indian administrators, including Napier, outlawed *suttee*, the practice of burning a man's wives alive on his funeral pyre. It was this sort of interference which contributed to the Indian Mutiny.

The revenge the British took on their Indian subjects after the Mutiny was atrocious, but it was demanded and endorsed by popular outcry in England, not by the then Governor General. He was nicknamed 'Clemency' Canning and execrated for his attempts to mitigate the savagery of the relieving troops. On the other hand, during the Famine in Ireland, it was a 'liberal', Charles Trevelyan, brought up in the very bosom of the Clapham Sect, who added to the misery by refusing to import enough emergency corn. In India Trevelyan was a reformer, in England he was later responsible for reforms to the army, but to Ireland he was like a Victorian family tyrant. The Irish were colonial subjects but they were also, confusingly, white and ought to have known better than to starve. They must not be encouraged to abandon responsibility for themselves to their rich relations. The Famine was another aspect of British imperial behaviour which I failed to find room for in my play.

Perhaps the most telling example of the division in British opinion between the humanitarians and the rest was the case of Governor Eyre and the negro rebellion in Jamaica. This happened after the abolition of slavery and soon after the Indian Mutiny. It will come into my second play and it's enough to say now that Eyre put down the rebellion with unnecessary ferocity, partly because the British in general feared another Mutiny elsewhere, partly because he was personally a kind of Basil Fawlty. This time the outcry in England came from the humanitarians led by J. S. Mill, Thomas Hughes and T. H. Huxley, who formed the 'Jamaica Committee' to prosecute Eyre for murder. He had already been recalled by the Government after a commission of inquiry had established that the rebellion – a small and local affair, though of course it might have got bigger if Eyre had not cracked down – had not justified the severity of the authorities' reaction. The Jamaica Committee was composed mainly of scientists (including Darwin, whose *Origin of Species* was still freshly controversial), academics and radical MPs, but included also clergymen and businessmen. It was what one might call now the 'Guardian lobby' and indeed one of its members, Thomas Bayley Potter, MP, was the son and nephew of the founders of The Manchester Guardian. Meanwhile on the opposite side was formed the 'Eyre

Defence Fund', whose committee included Carlyle (a rabid racist), Dickens, Ruskin, Sir Roderick Murchison (President of the Royal Geographical Society) and to which Tennyson contributed. The division was between non-conformism and the established Church, between radical and conservative politics (it was noticed and held against them by many at the time that the leadership of the Jamaica Committee was more or less identical with the leadership of the campaign for universal suffrage), between the idea of a democratic and beneficent Empire and what we would now (though they didn't then) call 'imperialism'. Huxley's famous sentence still bears witness to the whole 'good' side of the Empire. He considered it irrelevant whether Eyre acted from high motives or his chief victim from low (in fact the latter took no part in the rebellion), since 'English law does not permit good persons, as such, to strangle bad persons, as such' and he attacked the 'hero-worshippers who believe that the world is to be governed by its great men, who are to lead the little ones, justly if they can; but if not, drive or kick them the right way'.

The prosecution of Eyre failed and from then on the humanitarian side, for all it included Gladstone – whose unwilling imperialist action in Egypt was actually the signal for all the European land-grabbing in Africa of the nineties – gradually lost control of the Empire. In effect, the comparatively simple left-right politics of Britain itself got swamped by European politics, which were themselves partly affected by Britain's imperial role which in turn, as a result of European politics, took on a genuinely 'imperialist' dimension. I shall try to wrestle with this vicious circle in *The British Empire, Part Two*.

But although Part One deals with what I see as the Empire's 'innocence', it is not, I'm afraid, a pretty tale. I may have disposed of the traditional villain of the piece, or at least shown that he didn't mean to be a villain, but I have not thereby disposed of the villainy. The Tasmanians are chivvied and cosseted into extinction, the Afghans invaded, the Zulus started on their road to serfdom, the Indians made to lick up the blood of Cawnpore. The British for their part are murdered singly or in droves, brutalized, humiliated, driven to treachery, despair and suicide. Judged by its content, the play is a history, judged by its theme, a tragedy. Apologists for the Empire will say that I've left out all the good things that happened, the cultural, civilizing things that were done. It's true that I have – or only referred to them in passing – but the fact is that if you read the books you can't help being overwhelmed by the horrors. When our former colonies have got as far away from our Empire as we have from Rome's, perhaps it will all look to have been worthwhile, or at least neutral, something that for better or worse just happened and is now part of history. It is because it is not yet really history that I have written a tragedy. These people are still us, their world is still ours. We may not be responsible for the particular horrors enumerated here, but we know them from our screens and newspapers if not from actual experience. When I wrote the Afghan scenes I was thinking of Vietnam; by the time the play was performed history had repeated itself more exactly. The direct outcome of the South African scenes is still to come, probably in our time. When I deal with Arabi Pasha's rebellion in Part Two I shall be chronicling an earlier Nasser and a British Suez adventure which succeeded; the Mahdi and his dervishes will seem extraordinarily familiar to a world which has grown used to the Ayatollah Khomeini and his.

If the play is unusual it is because it became in the writing – I didn't plan it that way, but simply followed my nose through the histories and biographies – a multiple tragedy. There is no single, grand figure whose fatal flaw carries him to disaster, but a series of lesser figures, whose small individual failings and setbacks combine to form a national or rather international disaster. Burton, for example, avoids Laing's callow mistakes – he doesn't travel with Laing's local ignorance or ludicrous vanity nor does he get his head cut off – but he ends up skewered by Speke and trussed by his wife Isabel and the fault is as much his as theirs. Colonel Arthur and George Augustus Robinson (the 'Conciliator') between them destroy the very people they meant to save. The act was done, incidentally, mainly by persuading the aborigines to leave off their traditional grease and wear European clothes. The clothes got wet in Tasmania's drizzly climate, but it didn't occur to the aborigines to take them off and dry them. So they died rapidly of pneumonia. Letty Landon dies for her ignorance and insularity as surely as Laing or Macnaghten or the garrison of Cawnpore. Feringheea's betrayal of his people looks more like a good action than a bad, but what of Shaka's and Dingaan's? What above all of the Nana Sahib's? I have no historical evidence for his 'moral contortions'. I set out to make sense of his recorded actions and emerged with the Empire's Frankenstein monster. There is nothing to be said in favour of Colonel Neill or the Sergeant except that if you had seen the blood on the floor and the bodies in the well you might have behaved the same way. I think I would have behaved like the Subaltern, which is to say that I would have shepherded the Jews into

Auschwitz or the Cossacks into the train for Russia. I mean that I would have behaved that way at his age; I hope I wouldn't now.

As for economics, they have as little and as much to do with this story as, say, the fact that after Trafalgar, Britain ruled the seas or that the British saw the world as a hierarchy of peoples, with themselves as the divinely ordained upper crust. The effect of an early capitalist economy, then the most advanced in the world, on various kinds of more primitive economy, is the *sine qua non*, the basis of the drama, just as Thebes being a city-state with a 'classical economy' was the basis of *Oedipus Rex*, but it's not what the play is about. It would be deadly boring if it were, since everybody already knows that the British Empire was simply a question of economics. The play is about the superstructure of history and especially its moral element, but even that's putting it too theoretically. The play is about the characters, singly and collectively, and the characters are, for the sake of argument, our great-great-grandparents. They have a lot to answer for, but I hope the jury can find it in their hearts to be lenient, seeing that the accused didn't live in our enlightened century and that most of them have already paid fairly stiff penalties. Colonel Neill, incidentally, was killed shortly after his infamous edict, during the relief of Lucknow. The Sergeant and the Subaltern, I suspect, lived on into a shabby and nightmare-ridden old age and their great-great-grandchildren have no idea from whom they're descended.

John Spurling

SCENES AND CHARACTERS

1. *Trieste, 1884* Richard Burton, Isabel Burton.   1
2. *Kew Gardens, 1856* Richard Burton, Joseph Hooker.   4
3. *Central India, 1820.* 4 Indian Travellers.   8
4. *Tripoli, 1825* Emma Warrington, Gordon Laing, Mr. Warrington.   12
5. *Tasmania, 1828* Col. George Arthur, Tom.   16
6. *The Sahara, 1826* Gordon Laing, Sheikh Babani, Tuareg.   19
7. *Tasmania, 1830* Col. Arthur, Major Douglas, Captain Donaldson.   22
8. *Central India, 1828* Major Molony, Captain William Sleeman, Kalyan Singh.   25
9. *Tripoli, 1827* Emma Warrington.   28
10. *Zululand, 1824* Francis Farewell, Henry Fynn, Shaka, Jakot.   29
11. *Tasmania, 1830.* 3 Tasmanian Colonists.   34
12. *Central India, 1830* Feringheea, William Sleeman.   36
13. *Near Timbuctoo, 1826* Mobo, Gordon Laing, Sheikh Labeida.   40
14. *Downing Street, 1831* Lord Goderich, Lord Palmerston.   42
15. *Kew Gardens, 1856* Joseph Hooker, Richard Burton.   45
16. *Trieste, 1884* Richard Burton, Isabel Burton.   48
17. *Whitehall, 1839* Lord Palmerston, His Secretary.   51
18. *Tasmania, 1831* Col. Arthur, George Augustus Robinson.   56
19. *Hampstead Heath, 1836* Letty Landon, Captain George Maclean.   58
20. *Kabul, 1841* Sir William Macnaghten, Sir Alexander Burnes, Major-General William Elphinstone.   61
21. *Tasmania, 1832* George Augustus Robinson, Tasmanian Aborigines.   64
22. *Kabul, 1841* Maj.-Gen. Elphinstone, Sir William Macnaghten, Dr. Brydon, Captain Trevor.   66
23. *Zululand, 1835* Dingaan. Jakot, Allen Francis Gardiner.   70
24. *Cape Coast Castle, 1838* Letty Landon   73
25. *Kabul, 1841* Akbar Khan, Sir William Macnaghten, Capt. Trevor, Afghan Chiefs and Warriors.   76
26. *Flinders Island, Tasmania, 1838* George Augustus Robinson   79
27. *Zululand, 1835* Dingaan, Jakot, Allen Francis Gardiner.   81
28. *Jalalabad, 1842* Dr. Brydon, Capt. Sinclair, Capt. Cunningham.   86
29. *Kew Gardens, 1856* Richard Burton, Isabel Arundell.   88

30. *Tasmania, 1848* Mrs Clark, Robert Clark,
    Tasmanian Aborigines.   91
31. *Lucknow, 1857* Sir Henry Lawrence, Subahdar, Havildar,
    Sepoys.   93
32. *Tanganyika, 1858* Richard Burton, John Hanning Speke,
    Seedy Bombay.   96
33. *Cawnpore, 1857* Captain Moore, General Wheeler,
    Major Manning, Indian Woman, Sergeant, Havildar,
    Wounded man.   100
34. *Tanganyika, 1858* Richard Burton, John Speke,
    Seedy Bombay.   104
35. *Cawnpore, 1857* Nana Sahib, Azimulla, Tantia Topi.   107
36. *Tasmania, 1858* Bonwick, Dandridge.   111
37. *Cawnpore, 1857* Nana Sahib, Azimulla, Tantia Topi,
    Dancer.   114
38. *Tanganyika, 1858* Richard Burton, John Speke,
    Seedy Bombay.   118
39. *Cawnpore, 1857* Subaltern, Sergeant, Corporal Tanner,
    Evans, Jackson, Ramayan Sulin, Colonel Neill.   120
40. *Kew Gardens, 1859* Richard Burton, Isabel Arundell.   127
41. *Trieste, 1884* Richard Burton, Isabel Burton.   129

The general setting throughout is the Palm House at Kew.

The date and venue of each scene should be posted up at the side of the stage.

If the play is performed in its entirety and two intervals are needed, they are probably best placed after Scenes 15 and 28. If only one interval is needed, it should come after Scene 28.

THE BRITISH EMPIRE, PART ONE was first performed at the Birmingham Repertory Studio Theatre on February 14th, 1980, with the following cast:

EMMA WARRINGTON, LETTY LANDON, MRS CLARK
                                                                                  Jane Booker

RICHARD BURTON, WILLIAM SLEEMAN,
CAPTAIN MACLEAN, DR. BRYDON   David Howey

JOSEPH HOOKER, GENERAL ELPHINSTONE,
AKBAR KHAN, NANA SAHIB   Roger Hume

MR WARRINGTON, LORD GODERICH,
WILLIAM MACNAGHTEN, RAMAYAN SULIN   Ian Lindsay

COLONEL ARTHUR, CAPTAIN TREVOR,
JOHN HANNING SPEKE   Tony McHale

GORDON LAING, GEORGE AUGUSTUS ROBINSON,
AZIMULLA   Terry Molloy

ISABEL ARUNDELL, INDIAN WOMAN, BONWICK
                                                         Kate Percival

TOM, KALYAN SINGH, PALMERSTON'S SECRETARY,
TANTIA TOPI   Richard Rees

FERINGHEEA, LORD PALMERSTON, MR CLARK,
SEEDY BOMBAY   Leon Tanner

All other parts were played by the company.

The play was directed by Peter Farago

The play was designed by Poppy Mitchell
The lighting was by Charlie Paton

The scene with the Indian travellers, the three Zululand scenes and the scene at Lucknow were omitted from the Birmingham production. The scenes at Trieste were added later for the radio version of the play. They also make a better link with THE BRITISH EMPIRE, PART TWO.

THE BRITISH EMPIRE
PART ONE

Scene 1. Trieste 1884.

RICHARD BURTON, *British Consul in Trieste, is seated at a large table strewn with books and papers. He is 63, a tall man, but thin and wasted from the effects of a recent heart attack and suffering also from gout. With his head in his hands he reads, half aloud, from the manuscript in front of him.*

OLD BURTON: 'In the name of Allah, the Compassionating, the Compassionate!'

    ISABEL BURTON, *aged 53, a large matron with a heavy face, tightly dressed in black, enters softly.*

'The Beneficent King, the Creator of the Universe, Lord of the Three Worlds, Who set up the Firmament without Pillars in its stead and Who stretched out the Earth even as a Bed.' Isabel?

OLD ISABEL: Were you praying, Richard?

OLD BURTON: Not to your damned Pope and his virgin wife and mother.

OLD ISABEL: I know you do pray, whatever you may say to wound me. I've seen you on your knees.

OLD BURTON: Today is April the First. A suitable day for praying. Besides you may notice that I'm not on my knees, but seated at my table, as of yore, with thirty years' accumulation of notes and papers at my elbows.

OLD ISABEL: Isn't it too soon, Richard?

OLD BURTON: I'm sixty-three years old. It may be too late, but nothing can be too soon for Her Majesty's superannuated consul in Trieste. Except death.

OLD ISABEL: You nearly were dead. How did you even get yourself to the table without my help?

OLD BURTON: By the same means as I got myself to other inaccessible places in the days of my youth and strength. By desire. This table is now my Mecca and my lake regions of Central Africa.

OLD ISABEL: Don't speak as if I had been keeping you from it, You know that in all the world there's only ever been one person who wanted for you what you wanted for yourself. 'Love, honour and obey, in sickness and in health' – that was God's commandment. 'Pay, pack and follow' – that was your own. I dare anyone to say that I have strayed from those two commandments by a hair's breadth for twenty-three years. Your terrible illness has been your goaler these last months and before that the shameful spite and neglect of the authorities. I desperately want you to go back to work, Richard, but I also want you to finish your work, not collapse under the strain.

OLD BURTON: Everything is as you say, Isabel. You saved me once from despair. I have owed the best part of my life to you ever since. You'll have to help me again now. Most of the work has been done over the years. It's only the putting together. You must do the writing down, as usual, in your legible handwriting. Bring a chair and we'll begin.

She brings a chair, gathers fresh paper and a pen, and sits down.

OLD ISABEL: 'In the name of Allah, the Compassionating, the Compassionate . . .' No, you weren't praying, were you? *The Arabian Nights!* Isn't that too ambitious?

OLD BURTON: God's teeth! Can't you understand that it's now or never? Are you ready?

OLD ISABEL: Pay, pack and follow.

OLD BURTON: *(suddenly bursts out laughing)* But never without an argument first. 'Verily the works and words of those gone before us . . .'

She writes to his dictation

'... have become instances and examples to men of our modern day, that folk may view what admonishing chances befel other folk and may therefrom take warning; and that they may peruse the annals of antique peoples and all that hath betided them, and be thereby ruled and restrained...'

Scene 2. Kew Gardens 1856.

RICHARD BURTON, *now aged 35, and* JOSEPH DALTON HOOKER *stroll in from different sides, examining the plants in the Palm House. They are about the same height, but* BURTON *is much more powerfully built, with a Romantic, piratical face, prominently scarred on the cheek, and an immense moustache hanging down well below his chin.* HOOKER *is 39. He speaks with a Scottish intonation, having been brought up and educated in Glasgow, though he is not a Scot.* BURTON *seems to be looking for the label at the base of a palm-tree.*

HOOKER: *Palma reclinata.* He's an African.

BURTON: *(grunts)*

HOOKER: *Sabal blackburniana* – he's from the West Indies. *Archontophoenix cunninghamiana* – he's a mouthful, Australian. They all have their history. Somebody brought them home to England, each one lovingly from strange places. Perhaps if you were to count them, you'd find that for every man there's a plant. For every man that went out and never returned, an alien plant came home and survives at Kew.

BURTON: I take it you're a scientist, not a poet.

HOOKER: Rhododendron is my speciality. Forty-three species I've brought home from the Himalayas. And how they flourish! I wonder if I haven't done more by that simple act to change the face of England than anyone else to change the face of India.

BURTON: *(laughs)*

HOOKER: The life of plants is a perpetual struggle for the monopoly of the soil. Every modification of climate, every disturbance of the ground, every interference with the existing vegetation favours some species at the expense of others.

BURTON: And the same presumably for animals.

HOOKER: Why do you say that?

BURTON: It occurred to me.

HOOKER: My dearest friend is a geologist and naturalist. Charles Darwin. You don't happen to have met him?

BURTON: No.

HOOKER: Or heard a whisper about the book he's working on? No? Great minds think alike.

BURTON: But if plants and animals, then I suppose men too?

HOOKER: Don't ask me about *homo sapiens*. Morality intervenes there, with incalculable consequences. Especially in our century, especially in the Empire. It's not all Palmerston and the strong arm, is it? It's also Wilberforce and the soft conscience. Freeing the slaves was only the most obvious interference with the old order of things. We have set a race of Galahads galloping through the world's wildernesses in search of the Grail. The sense of adventure! Moral improvement! Science has no way of measuring their effects. *Palma sylvestris* – the wild date of India.

BURTON: Yes. I spent seven years in India.

HOOKER: Well, I knew that.

BURTON: By my complexion?

HOOKER: By your moustache and your scar. You've also been to Mecca disguised as an Arab. You came by your scar at Berbera, among the Somalis. Captain Burton, no?

BURTON: Salaam!

HOOKER: I've read your adventures with baited breath.

BURTON: And you?

HOOKER: Joseph Hooker.

BURTON: Author of *Flora Antarctica* and *Flora Indica*.

HOOKER: You've read them?

BURTON: Not yet.

HOOKER: Didn't you also fight with Napier in Sind?

BURTON: I was posted to Sind after the fighting was over. Likewise I missed the reconquest of Afghanistan. Likewise when it came to the Sikh Wars and the conquest of the Punjab, though I applied to go as an interpreter, I was turned down. The authorities preferred a Lieutenant XYZ who spoke Hindustani to Lieutenant Burton who spoke Hindustani, Gujarati, Punjabi, Sindhee, Maharatee, Persian and Arabic and was besides the best swordsman, marksman and horseman in the Indian Army.

HOOKER: Someone is saving you for better things.

BURTON: Someone has decided that I'm not to be given the chance of military glory.

HOOKER: Well, nobody will be doing much fighting in the near future. Afghanistan, Sind, the Punjab, and now Oudh – the whole of India has been taken under British rule.

BURTON: British rule in India is doomed. There will be a massacre.

HOOKER: Surely not? We are infinitely preferable to their old rulers. Corruption, torture, armed robbery, religious oppression, tribal wars – all done away with. Now they have canals and roads, equal justice before the law, peace from one end of India to the other.

BURTON: Imposed by barbarians. That's how the Indians think of us. Insolent, ignorant, irreligious hooligans. They long to drive us out.

HOOKER: Is anyone but you aware of this?

BURTON: The Directors of the East India Company, if they've taken the trouble to read the letter I wrote them.

HOOKER: Do you expect it to make any difference?

BURTON: None at all. I only wrote the letter for the pleasure of telling them what I thought of them.

HOOKER: You may have damaged your career.

BURTON: That was done already. Napier employed me in Sind to gather intelligence. After his retirement one of my reports found its way from his private drawer to the desk of the Governor of Bombay. From there, swift as fate, to the old men in Leadenhall Street. I was sent down from Oxford for attending a horse race. Now you might say I've been sent down from India.

HOOKER: Dear me! What was the subject of your report.

BURTON: The male brothels of Karachi. I went into some detail. I discovered, for example, that boys are preferred to eunuchs. On account of the scrotum. I too am a scientist in my fashion, Mr. Hooker. I believe that everything in the world is there to be examined. I believe the truth is all that counts. How is a country to be well governed unless its most intimate truths are known to the governors?

HOOKER: Where next? If you can't go back to India?

BURTON: Africa. The Mountains of the Moon and the source of the Nile.

HOOKER: My dear fellow!

BURTON: At least there'll be no sahibs there, or worse still, memsahibs.

HOOKER: You're like a bee.

BURTON: You think I'm not serious?

HOOKER: Bees are very serious creatures. They carry pollen, they propagate. Where you go, the sahibs and memsahibs will be sure to follow . . .

They stroll off together.

Scene 3. Central India. 1820.

An elderly Indian, hot and dusty from travelling, enters and sits down. He begins to cook chapatties. Two younger Indians, also travellers, enter and put down their bundles nearby.

FIRST YOUNG INDIAN: A hot day!

OLD INDIAN: Very hot. God be praised for the man who planted this grove of trees!

SECOND YOUNG INDIAN: A charitable action. He was thinking of poor travellers like ourselves. Have you come far?

OLD INDIAN: Have I come far? All the way from Benares.

SECOND INDIAN: A pilgrim?

OLD INDIAN: Oh yes.

FIRST INDIAN: The roads are dangerous. Robbers everywhere.

OLD INDIAN: God be praised, I'm too poor to tempt robbers.

FIRST INDIAN: Is that any protection? People who have to carry treasure dress up to look poor.

OLD INDIAN: Well...

SECOND INDIAN: How would the robbers know the difference between you and one of them?

FIRST INDIAN: I daresay you're a local man. Friends in the district?

OLD INDIAN: Oh no.

SECOND INDIAN: You've far to go?

OLD INDIAN: Have I far to go? It will be two months before I get near my home.

FIRST INDIAN: You have some friends along the way?

OLD INDIAN: No one. I can only put my trust in God.

FIRST INDIAN: It's lucky we've met.

SECOND INDIAN: Safety in numbers.

> *All three settle down to eat. Enter another youngish Indian.*

THIRD INDIAN: Hot day!

SECOND INDIAN: Very hot. God be praised for the man who planted this grove of trees to shade travellers!

THIRD INDIAN: You've seen no robbers?

FIRST INDIAN: What makes you say that?

SECOND INDIAN: Are there robbers?

FIRST INDIAN: We're too poor to be robbed. That's this old man's opinion.

OLD INDIAN: We can only trust in God.

FIRST INDIAN: Why don't you sit down with us? The more the merrier when we're all strangers far from home.

THIRD INDIAN: None of you has any friends in the district?

SECOND INDIAN: No. We're on our way to Allahabad and this old man has been to Benares. His home is still two months away.

FIRST INDIAN: Join us.

SECOND INDIAN: Safety in numbers.

> *THIRD INDIAN sits down and eats with them.*

OLD INDIAN: *(yawning)* It's late.

FIRST INDIAN: Shall we go on together in the morning?

THIRD INDIAN: Why not?

SECOND INDIAN: No need to sleep yet. It's so pleasant to sit here in peace among friends.

OLD INDIAN: God is kind to us.

FIRST INDIAN: Won't you sing us a pilgrim's song?

OLD INDIAN: My voice isn't what it was.

>*He clears his throat and begins to chant in a quaver.*

FIRST INDIAN: Let's chew tobacco!

Instantly, SECOND INDIAN seizes the OLD INDIAN'S arms, THIRD INDIAN his legs, while FIRST INDIAN puts a ruhmal (large knotted handkerchief) round his stretched neck and tightens it. OLD INDIAN struggles feebly, but the others throw him on his face, when FIRST INDIAN puts foot on his back and with a final jerk of the ruhmal strangles him.

FIRST INDIAN: Now cut the body and disjoint the knees. The grave is dug?

THIRD INDIAN: Just through the trees there.

FIRST INDIAN: First we'll see if he told the truth about his poverty.

>*They go through the old man's pockets and bundle and find a few small coins.*

>Nothing worth having. If the Goddess is kind we shall find a richer one tomorrow. Take it away!

>*SECOND AND THIRD INDIAN carry out the body while FIRST INDIAN delves in bundle and brings out gur (consecrated sugar), the sacred pick-axe and a flask of water. The others return and all kneel round a small hole scooped in the ground.*

FIRST INDIAN: *(putting a little gur into the hole and clasping hands in prayer)* Great Goddess Bhowani, as thou didst vouchsafe one lac of rupees to Joora Naig and Koduk Bunwaree in their need, so we pray thee, fulfil our desires!

He sprinkles water over the sacred pick-axe and gives a little gur *to each of the others to hold in their hands.*

FIRST INDIAN: *(a hunting cry)* Let's chew tobacco!

OTHERS: Let's chew tobacco!

They eat their portions of gur *in silence. Distant noise of voices.*

FIRST INDIAN: *(hastily scooping everything into his bundle)* People are coming. Quickly now! We must fill in the grave and lay the bedrolls over it. We will sleep on that place.

They go out hurriedly.

Scene 4. Tripoli. 1825

Enter EMMA WARRINGTON, followed by GORDON LAING, aged 31, a slight, wiry figure, son of an Edinburgh schoolmaster.

EMMA: Yes, oh yes!

LAING: My darling Emma! *(he takes her hand and kisses it)*

Enter WARRINGTON, Emma's father, British consul in Tripoli.

WARRINGTON: Major Laing! How dare you?

EMMA: Father, we're in love.

WARRINGTON: Nonsense, Emma. Go to your room! Major Laing is about to leave for Timbuctoo. He has no time to be in love.

EMMA: He's just asked me to marry him.

WARRINGTON: What have you to say for yourself, Laing?

LAING: I have the honour, sir, to ask for your daughter's hand in marriage.

WARRINGTON: Refused! Categorically refused!

EMMA: No, father!

LAING: On what grounds, Mr. Warrington?

WARRINGTON: All grounds. You've abused my hospitality. My official position as British consul in Tripoli. You've only been here a week. You arrive out of the blue on your way to nowhere and you expect to marry my daughter! Have you abandoned the discovery of Timbuctoo? Or was that a mere excuse to insinuate yourself into my house and turn my daughter's silly head?

LAING: I resent that!

EMMA: So do I. We want to be married at once, before he goes into the desert.

WARRINGTON: Major Laing can go where he pleases, into the desert or to the moon. So long as he doesn't remain under my roof.

LAING: You think I'm unworthy of your daughter? A nobody?

WARRINGTON: I never said that. You came with Lord Bathurst's recommendation. Until this moment you showed yourself a person of some natural breeding.

LAING: I shall show myself what I have always considered myself. A man of enterprise. A man of genius.

WARRINGTON: That's not the point.

LAING: What is the point? You mean to ruin our lives because you'd hoped for a more conventional son-in-law?

WARRINGTON: Please, Laing, try to see it as I see it. Imagine yourself Emma's father and me a captain from a West African regiment . . .

LAING: A major.

WARRINGTON: A local major. Your rank is a temporary one.

LAING: It will be at least lieutenant-colonel when I return.

WARRINGTON: *If* you return. It's not a family outing. You're about to cross the Sahara desert *en route* for a mysterious and perhaps mythical city in the heart of an unknown continent. Would you allow a man who was about to cross the Sahara desert to marry your daughter?

LAING: You'll think yourself damned lucky to have married your daughter to the discoverer of Timbuctoo. And if I die in the attempt, you've lost nothing.

WARRINGTON: Lost nothing? What about Emma's happiness?

EMMA: He'll do it, father. He'll get there. I know he will.

LAING: I believe it is my destiny to discover Timbuctoo.

WARRINGTON: Very well, but it is not your destiny to marry my daughter. There is no one in Tripoli to perform the ceremony.

EMMA: But you're the British Consul. Consuls can perform marriages.

WARRINGTON: What? I'm not at all certain of that.

LAING: They've done so in the past.

WARRINGTON: But were the marriages valid? No, if there were any question of marriage, which is not the case, it would have to be done in Malta by a clergyman of the Church of England.

LAING: Now, look, I leave in two days. You must perform the ceremony, Warrington.

WARRINGTON: Now you look here, Laing! I have not even given my consent. I am certainly not going to perform the ceremony without my own consent.

EMMA: Father, be reasonable! This last week you have done nothing but admire Major Laing. You said yourself what courage he had – the sort of man, you said, that gave England her reputation in the world. How many more such men do you think exist? How many more are going to turn up in Tripoli? Suppose you send Major Laing into the desert, his mind distracted with unhappiness? Will history ever forgive you? I know I won't. You won't forgive yourself.

WARRINGTON: I will perform the ceremony. Under protest, on a temporary basis, and with one absolute condition: the marriage must not be consummated. Not until it can be confirmed in Malta. Do you understand me, Emma? You must remain within sight of your mother or myself at all times of day and night until Major Laing leaves for Timbuctoo.

LAING: Fair enough.

WARRINGTON: Emma?

EMMA: If it must be so.

WARRINGTON: It must. Now I shall go and inform your mother. She'll think me lunatic.

He is going out. LAING and EMMA touch hands. WARRINGTON turns back.

We will all go and inform your mother.

They go out.

Scene 5. Tasmania. 1828.

Enter COLONEL GEORGE ARTHUR, *Governor of Tasmania, aged 44. He is a small, alert, stiffly upright man, a martinet, with a pale, unsmiling, puritanical face. He sits at his desk and begins to go through a pile of papers.*

ARTHUR: John Kemp, speared to death by aborigines . . . Jack Baskett, two cows speared . . . Jones, Forest and M'Candless, speared to death . . .

He picks up a newspaper.

'In view of the rapidly worsening situation in the farming districts, it must be asked what the authorities propose to do to protect innocent men . . . Nothing effectual will be done till the tone of moderation is abandoned and the strong arm of power made use of.'

Puts down the newspaper and opens another.

'Mr. Andrew Bright recommends the use of poisoned flour. Mr. Hector McKay wonders why we can't import blacks from Sydney to hunt aborigines. Mr. John Lob demands that convicts be sent into the bush, with remission of sentence for every native killed or captured.'

He puts down the newspaper, gets up and paces about.

Yes, yes, yes. But who originated these murderous acts?

He returns to desk and finds another paper.

'A native woman, with her husband and another native, were tricked into boarding a small boat. Once in deep water, the boatmen threw the two male aborigines overboard. The woman was held in the bottom of the boat and forced to watch as her husband, a strong swimmer, clung to the boat's gunwale and cried for mercy. One of the boatmen then chopped off his hands.'

Tap on the door and enter TOM, *an aborigine dressed in*

European clothes.

TOM: Newspaper, Colonel Arthur, sah!

ARTHUR: Ah, Tom! I've been making some pictures. Come and look at them.

TOM: What dis?

ARTHUR: This is an aborigine and a white man. See, they have their arms round one another's shoulders. And here are their children playing together. Now in the next picture here is the governor with his soldiers . . .

TOM: Dat you? Don't look like you.

ARTHUR: It's my hat, see. The face is not so important, is it?

TOM: What you going to do to dese natives? Shoot dem?

ARTHUR: On the contrary. The governor and his soldiers are greeting them as friends.

TOM: Dat good. When dat been happen?

ARTHUR: Now in these two pictures we have a spot of bother.

TOM: Oh my hat! Dis poor native, he get hanged from de tree by him neck.

ARTHUR: Because he speared that white man, see? But now look at this picture.

TOM: Oh, dis terrible story! White man been shoot dis poor native dead.

ARTHUR: And the governor hangs him for it. Hangs the white man. You understand?

TOM shakes head over the sadness of the story.

ARTHUR: Now, Tom, I'm going to make many, many of these pictures and put them on boards and take them into the forest and nail them up to trees. So that the aborigines can understand that I want to make friends with them. Don't you think that a good idea?

TOM: What? You go make proflamation to native? Ha, ha! I never see dat foolish. When he see dat? He can't read dat. Who tell him?

ARTHUR: What about you, Tom? Will you go and tell him for me?

TOM: Me? No. Me like see you tell him yourself. He very soon spear me.

ARTHUR walks about, deep in thought.

TOM: Newspaper, sah.

He puts newspaper on the desk and goes out. ARTHUR absently picks up newspaper, then notices the headline and reads in haste.

ARTHUR: 'Outrage at Oatlands... Scene of horror and tragedy... Whole family speared by marauding savages. Now at last the Governor must act.'

He throws down the newspaper.

Action we shall have. A campaign. The most meticulously planned campaign ever fought by a British army in the field. We shall solve this problem at one sweep! To work!

Gathering up all his papers he goes out.

Scene 6. The Sahara. 1826.

Night. LAING is seated on his camp-bed inside his tent, writing a letter.

LAING: 'Latitude 23°N. Dear Warrington, we are proceeding at 20 miles a day over a desert of sand as flat as a bowling green. Our caravan, after so many difficulties and delays, has now had the luck to fall in with a party of Tuaregs. They've taken us under their protection. No doubt my own fame as the first free Christian ever to appear in these parts makes them feel honoured to do so. *(slight sound from outside)* Sheikh Babani?

Enter SHEIKH BABANI, LAING's guide.

BABANI: Permission to disturb, sir. This is the problem: Tuaregs expect an attack tomorrow.

LAING: They promised to protect us.

BABANI: That is their earnest desire. Problem being they have run short of gunpowder. If you were to give them yours...

LAING: I'll need it myself.

BABANI: No, sir, they will protect you. But not without gunpowder. This is dilemma we are facing.

LAING: I dislike the idea.

BABANI: Tuaregs prefer to ride away and be far from scene than incur dishonour of not being able to protect you in case of disaster.

LAING: Why did they offer protection if they've not the means to ensure it?

BABANI: No. Insufficient means, in view of threat now expected.

LAING: You mean I've no alternative, if I want them to stay?

BABANI: This is heart of problem.

LAING: *(handing over key)* Give it them, then, Sheikh Babani.

BABANI: Now all can sleep soundly. Whole caravan will call blessing on you, sir. Goodnight!

He goes out. LAING continues letter.

LAING: 'As for Lord Bathurst's complaints about the cost of my expedition, you can tell him he'll hear no more from me on the subject of money. Sheikh Babani, the guide supplied me by the Pasha of Tripoli, has already been paid handsomely in advance. He is an idle rogue and deserves no more. I shall continue to submit quarterly statements to the Colonial and Audit Offices . . .'

He throws down pen and slaps his thigh with repressed fury.

Good God! I never came here for money and Lord Bathurst knows it. How can he begin to reward me for what I've already been through? No doubt he thinks it will be enough to make me up to Lieutenant-Colonel. I won't accept it. This world is made of such commonplace matter that it's painful for a purpose of mind to exist in it.

Another slight noise outside.

Sheikh Babani?

Returns to letter.

'It gives me some pleasure to look at the improvement I've already made in the map of Africa. You must keep up my dear Emma's spirits. Never fear, I shall come through safely . . .

Shots are fired into the tent from outside. LAING falls, wounded in the side. He is trying to reach his gun, when a TUAREG enters, attacks him with a scimitar and wounds his right arm, his face, head, hands and neck. TUAREG then removes any valuables he can find and goes out, leaving LAING bleeding on the floor. Enter BABANI.

BABANI: Oh, sir, we should never have trusted their silky words.

They have only attacked our part of caravan. Remainder of caravan now striking tents and impatient to be gone, fearing villains may strike again. I myself will go with caravan, not to lose sight. You and camel-driver must follow as soon as convenient. He is also wounded. Camel is unhurt.

He goes out. LAING crawls painfully after him.

Scene 7. Tasmania. 1830.

Enter ARTHUR, carrying a huge stack of papers, followed by MAJOR DOUGLAS and CAPTAIN DONALDSON.

ARTHUR: *(laying papers on table)* Gentlemen, this year we shall solve the native problem. A map. *(finds and unrolls it on desk)* The heart of the problem is boundaries, at present ill-defined. We shall therefore move the natives into a reserved part of the island where they will be free to roam unmolested through the virgin bush – an essential ingredient of their way of life – leaving the colonists to improve and cultivate the rest of the island. Here is the reserve, gentlemen, created by Providence for our purpose. The Tasman Peninsula. We have but to place the natives there, close up the neck with guard-posts and *ipso facto* peace reigns. Any questions?

DONALDSON: It's a brilliant scheme, sir.

DOUGLAS: Brilliant. I have one question. How easy will it be to persuade the natives to make the move?

DONALDSON: I suppose it's simply a matter of finding the chaps, here and there in the bush, and alerting them where to make for. The Peninsula.

ARTHUR: If it were as simple as that, Captain Donaldson, I could have spared myself many long days and nights of toil. We shall have to drive them there.

DOUGLAS: Drive them? The whole native population?

ARTHUR: As one drives game.

DOUGLAS: But the area involved is at least a hundred square miles.

ARTHUR: We shall need a cordon of some length –120 miles at the start, contracting as we near our goal. We shall employ three regiments of soldiers and an auxiliary force of civilian volunteers.

DONALDSON: The terrain is terrible, sir. Some of the bush virtually impenetrable and the land's all broken up into ravines and gullies. Not easy going.

ARTHUR: It has not been easy going drawing up the plans for this campaign.

He hands papers to officers.

In this paper you will find precise details of the signals to be used up and down the line. Details of rations are in this paper and location of supply-points in this one.

DOUGLAS: You say here, sir, that each man in the cordon is to be sixty yards from his neighbour. With all respect, sir, I don't think this kind of exactitude is obtainable in the bush.

ARTHUR: It is obtainable if the will is there, Major Douglas. *(hands out more papers)* These are the details of clothing and equipment. They're divided into military and civilian.

DONALDSON: How many civilians do you envisage?

ARTHUR: Two thousand or so. *(hands out more papers)* Now for weapons. No killing whatever is the order and I want it observed to the letter unless any man is actually in danger of his life.

DOUGLAS: Hard to restrain civilians from banging away on the slightest pretext.

ARTHUR: That had occurred to me. Only certain civilians will bear arms. In case of emergency, I shall set up a central reserve of arms and ammunition at Oatlands. Three hundred pairs of handcuffs will also be available.

DONALDSON: For the natives or the civilians?

ARTHUR: For anyone that needs restraining, Donaldson.

DOUGLAS: What is the date of starting, sir?

ARTHUR: All successful military campaigns are fought between seed-time and harvest-time. Ours will be no exception. Operation 'Black Drive' will commence the 7th of October. Thank you, gentlemen, you will receive more detailed instructions in due course. I have now to brief the editor of the Hobart Town Gazette. Good morning!

He goes out with remaining papers, followed by the two officers.

Scene 8. Central India. 1828.

Enter MAJOR MOLONY and CAPTAIN WILLIAM SLEEMAN. Sleeman, a Stocky Cornishman, is 40 and Molony somewhat older.

MOLONY: You won't get any pig-sticking here, Sleeman. But we're glad to have you. Always the same when the Company takes over new territory. What you find under the stones is nobody's business. Hundreds of years of bad government to be put right before you can even think of running a smooth administration. We're bloody hard-pressed.

SLEEMAN: Who are all these people waiting outside your office?

MOLONY: We're going to have to let them go. Supposed to be in possession of stolen goods, but not a scrap of evidence. No one has come forward to claim anything.

SLEEMAN: Perhaps the victims are all dead.

MOLONY: Then where are the bodies?

SLEEMAN: When I first landed in Calcutta – twenty years ago – I came across a travel-book written by a Frenchman in the 17th century. He described a special sort of robbers, called 'deceivers' – 'Thugs' is the Indian word – who made friends with travellers and then strangled them and buried them.

MOLONY: Nothing's absolutely impossible in India.

SLEEMAN: Much later, in Allahabad, I was looking through the Collector's library and found a report, written twenty years ago by an English surgeon. He suggested the Thugs had existed for centuries and were something like a religious fellowship.

MOLONY: Religious? Wouldn't you know it? This country's rotten with religion. Whatever people may say against the Company, at least it doesn't allow Christian missionaries in India. That would be the final straw.

SLEEMAN: I happen to be Christian myself.

MOLONY: Aren't we all? But quite frankly a bit of honest-to-goodness atheism would do wonders for this country.

SLEEMAN: Suppose there were this secret society, this hidden growth spreading all over India! Suppose one could put a hand on one branch of it, mightn't it be possible to follow that down to the root, dig the whole thing up?

MOLONY: Your court-house is over there.

SLEEMAN: You think it's a fairy-tale?

MOLONY: Everyone has his pet obsession. With some it's promotion, with others it's tigers or astrology or, God help us, billiards. You don't drink, do you? That's the main thing. See you in the club about half past twelve!

> MOLONY *claps* SLEEMAN *on the shoulder and goes out.* SLEEMAN *starts to go the other way.* KALYAN SINGH *enters and follows him stealthily.* SLEEMAN *stops.*

SLEEMAN: What do you want?

KALYAN: You are not remembering me, Sleeman Sahib? Kalyan Singh.

SLEEMAN: I think so.

KALYAN: You were sending me to prison last year. In Narsinghpore.

SLEEMAN: I remember you only too well. You'd been thieving.

KALYAN: You are remembering me, Sahib, because you were taking care of my little boy.

SLEEMAN: You're in bad company again, Kalyan Singh. Weren't you with those men outside Molony Sahib's office?

KALYAN: (*lowering voice and looking about guiltily*) You know those men?

SLEEMAN: I know they're criminals.

KALYAN: Their leader especially so. A hard, cruel, evil man.

SLEEMAN: He's not given you your share of the takings.

KALYAN: Sahib, you look into men's hearts.

SLEEMAN: What do you want to tell me?

KALYAN: *(looks about, moves further off, beckons SLEEMAN after him)* Thugs. You understand me, Sahib?

SLEEMAN: *(taking his arm)* This way! Quickly!

KALYAN: What are you doing?

SLEEMAN: Taking you straight to jail. For your own safety. I can't afford to lose you.

They go out.

Scene 9. Tripoli. 1827.

Enter EMMA. She takes an old letter, much folded, out of her bosom and reads it over in a low, expressionless voice.

EMMA: 'Dear Warrington, I have altogether twenty-four wounds, eighteen of them very severe. Five sabre cuts on the top of the head and three on the left temple; one on the left cheek which fractured the jaw-bone and divided the ear – an unsightly wound. One over the right temple. A nasty gash on the back of the neck which slightly scratched the windpipe. A bullet in the hip which made its way through the back and slightly grazed the backbone. Five sabre cuts on the right arm and hand, three of the fingers broken. The hand cut three-quarters across and the wrist-bones severed. Three cuts on the left arm, the bone broken but mending. One slight wound on the right leg and two, plus a nasty gash, on the left leg. The cut across the fingers of the left hand has healed. I'm doing well and have collected some important geographical information. The details of my feverish camel-ride through the desert for four hundred miles in the wake of the caravan which had left me for dead must wait for another occasion. My kindest love to Emma and tell her to think nothing of my misfortune. All will be well. I move on now towards Timbuctoo . . .'

She folds the letter slowly, then bursts into tears.

Oh, Major Laing, Major Laing, but that was a year ago! Where are you now?

She goes out.

Scene 10. Zululand. 1824.

The interior of SHAKA's hut. In the centre, a grand armchair. Enter LIEUTENANT FRANCIS GEORGE FAREWELL, RN, 33, now director of a trading company, and HENRY FRANCIS FYNN, 21. In the distance a continual wailing and the sound of regular blows, as of someone hitting a sack.

FAREWELL: What do you think of the chair?

FYNN: Nice.

FAREWELL: Will he appreciate it?

FYNN: Bound to.

FAREWELL: *(sitting in chair)* Not bad at all, is it? I got it from Capetown. They were refurnishing Government House. Cost almost nothing. What is that beastly noise?

FYNN: They're punishing Shaka's assassins. Would-be assassins. Alleged would-be assassins.

FAREWELL: Tell me about Shaka. Is he fully recovered?

FYNN: More or less. It was a nasty wound.

FAREWELL: Near thing?

FYNN: Very near. He was very frightened.

FAREWELL: But you made him better. You saved his life.

FYNN: It was just a question of keeping the wound clean and talking him over his fright.

FAREWELL: Henry Francis Fynn, you're a bloody fine fellow. You're a hero. *(waves paper)* Now I've drawn up a document, all legal and proper, for Shaka to grant us land round Port Natal. This is going to be the making of the company. We can settle down, build houses and warehouses, put our trade with the Zulus on a firm footing and, generally speaking, plant the flag.

FYNN: It may not be as easy as that.

FAREWELL: Why not? You mean the Government won't let us plant the flag. But at least if we've got a fair and square treaty with Shaka they'll have to recognise our existence.

FYNN: Not the Government. Here. We've got Jaket to deal with.

FAREWELL: That damned Xhosa cattle-thief? What's he got to do with it? He isn't even a Zulu.

FYNN: He's set himself up as Shaka's European expert and any dealings with Shaka have to go through him.

FAREWELL: Surely they've finished beating those bloody assassins by now?

FYNN: Nowhere near. The whole population of the kraal is queuing up to take a turn.

FAREWELL: How are we going to fix Jakot?

FYNN: No way. He's got a grudge against us.

FAREWELL: We'll have to rattle him.

FYNN: What use will that be?

FAREWELL: I don't know. But if there's some bugger getting in your light when you want to pull off a deal, it sometimes helps to make him lose his temper. A good tip, that.

SHAKA and JAKOT appear at the entrance to the hut. SHAKA, still bandaged round the arm and chest, leans a little on JAKOT.

SHAKA: Is that the present they've brought me? A throne.

JAKOT: A chair.

SHAKA: A King's chair.

JAKOT: They have plenty of chairs like that at Capetown. And better.

>   FAREWELL *bows and gestures towards chair.* SHAKA *goes and sits in it.*

FAREWELL: I hope that King Shaka is happy with this magnificent throne which King George has sent him. In return, and because we know that King Shaka is grateful that his life was saved by an English doctor and English medicine, we ask him to make us a small gift of land. This treaty...

JAKOT: Do you think King Shaka is a fool, Mr. Farewell? Where do I come from? I am a Xhosa. The Xhosas had land once, like the Zulus. Where is it now? Boers took it, British took it. I was a chief of Xhosas.

FAREWELL: A chief? Come off it! You were a thief. A cattle-thief.

JAKOT: My own cattle! My own cattle taken by Boer thiefs!

FAREWELL: This is old history. Ask King Shaka to give us the land and sign this treaty.

JAKOT: I will never see Zulus treated like Xhosas. King Shaka gave me my own kraal, own cattle, own wives. Zulu people my people. No land! Never!

FAREWELL: *(handing treaty to* FYNN*)* Give it to Shaka.

FYNN: *(he does so)* Please!

SHAKA: What is this? Another present?

JAKOT: Throw it away! It's nothing.

SHAKA: If it's nothing, why did he give it to me?

JAKOT: They're asking for land. In return for that chair.

SHAKA: I like this chair.

JAKOT: Not a very wonderful chair.

SHAKA: I have a lot of land.

JAKOT: Don't give it for a chair. Give some small present if you want to. A few cattle, a few wives, but not land.

SHAKA: Land is cheap.

JAKOT: Listen! First come people like this, traders asking for land. They are given it and ask for more. Next come the missionaries and ask for land to build churches. Missionaries are worse than traders. They make trouble among your people. Last come soldiers and take all the land, without asking. Believe me!

SHAKA: Are you trying to frighten me? I am not a man to be frightened.

JAKOT: Your sickness frightened you.

SHAKA: Who are you? What do you know? You tell me what happened to some broken-down tribes at the edge of my kingdom. Are you giving this woman's advice to me, the King of the Zulus? You think these people's soldiers are better than mine? You think I haven't the power to give my land as I please? *(He stands up)* Can these men give me a throne? No, only a chair. But I, because I sit in it, make this chair a throne. Now, if I am afraid to give them land, what then? Then they can give me a throne, because they must be greater than I am.

FAREWELL: What's going on? Shaka doesn't want to lose his chair?

FYNN: Jakot may have played the wrong card.

> SHAKA *groans, clutches his chest and sits down. FYNN hurries across and fiddles with the bandages.*

SHAKA: Ask them how much land they want.

JAKOT: What have you written in your paper?

FAREWELL: Most of it is just ceremony, friendship, our great desire to trade with Shaka and his people . . .

JAKOT: How much land?

FAREWELL: All we ask is the land round Port Natal.

JAKOT: How much?

FAREWELL: Twenty-five miles along the sea. One hundred miles inwards from the sea. A small strip.

JAKOT: They're asking for as much land as a great chief. Let it be one quarter.

SHAKA: Tell them that my gratitude is not sufficiently expressed by this small gift of land and that I shall give them besides as much cattle and corn as they desire. They are to send my greetings to my brother, their own king um George.

JAKOT: *(to FAREWELL)* You have got it.

FAREWELL: Please convey our deep thanks to King Shaka for his generosity. *(to FYNN, handing him pen)* Get his mark on it.

JAKOT: *(to SHAKA)* This is a bad day for Zulus.

SHAKA, helped by FYNN, makes his mark on treaty, then get to his feet and goes out, leaning on FYNN. As he goes, FYNN hands treaty to FAREWELL.

FAREWELL: *(making thumbs up sign)* We're in business.

He goes out, smiling at JAKOT.

Scene 11. Tasmania. 1830.

Enter three COLONISTS limping in a line, one behind the other. All wear tattered clothes and ruined boots. They are wet and stooped, forcing their way through thick bush, slipping and sliding in mud.

SECOND COLONIST: Oh mother!

THIRD COLONIST: Fucking father!

SECOND COLONIST: Did you bring me into the world to die of exhaustion on a bleeding kangaroo track?

THIRD COLONIST: Did you ever think your son would grow up to be a wet rag in a sodding Tasmanian thorn-bush?

SECOND COLONIST: How do they expect me to see an abo when I can't see my own fucking feet?

THIRD COLONIST: Governor bleeding Arthur is the only one I want to see.

SECOND COLONIST: Send him to a blasted offshore island.

FIRST COLONIST: You stupid bastards! If Governor Arthur sees you following me, he'll have you for his bloody breakfast.

SECOND COLONIST: If the kangaroos can't get through any other way, how do you expect me to?

FIRST COLONIST: Do you call this a cordon? Sixty yards apart?

THIRD COLONIST: Somebody should put a cordon round fucking Arthur.

SECOND COLONIST: Drop him off the Tasman Peninsula.

THIRD COLONIST: The lads down the line caught two abos.

FIRST COLONIST: They didn't?

THIRD COLONIST: A man and a boy. The man escaped.

SECOND COLONIST: They should have read the bloody paper.

FIRST COLONIST: What paper?

SECOND COLONIST: The Courier. Some cunt was telling us how to catch a native.

THIRD COLONIST: I've never even seen a fucking native.

SECOND COLONIST: If you do, they're covered in grease. You have to put your arms through his armpits.

THIRD COLONIST: Bloody hell!

SECOND COLONIST: Then you clasp your hands behind his neck and fucking overpower him.

THIRD COLONIST: Let me try it! Stand still, you prick! *(gets hold of FIRST COLONIST and follows instructions)* It works!

FIRST COLONIST: Lay off, for Christ's sake!

SECOND COLONIST: Of course it works. The only trouble is the bastards don't come and stand around two feet in front of you.

THIRD COLONIST: Come on, then! Another two hours and we can lie down for another fucking kip in the mud.

SECOND COLONIST: Roll on!

FIRST COLONIST: Get off my bloody path!

They straggle out.

Scene 12. Central India. 1830.

FERINGHEEA *is standing, manacled ankles to wrist, beside a desk. At the desk sits* SLEEMAN *studying a file, taking no notice of the prisoner. After some time he looks up, as if seeing* FERINGHEEA *for the first time.*

SLEEMAN: You have a complaint?

FERINGHEEA: What is this? British justice? Arresting an innocent man, chaining me like a criminal!

SLEEMAN: Feringheea! I have been hunting Thugs for two years now. Time and again I have sent men to bring you in. Time and again you've eluded me. During your last expedition you and your gang murdered one hundred and five women and children. You will hang. I don't imagine that Thuggee will end with your death, but by God it will help.

FERINGHEEA: There will never be an end of Thuggee.

SLEEMAN: Why do you do these things? Not apparently for money.

FERINGHEEA: You are not understanding Thuggee.

SLEEMAN: Then enlighten me! Listen, if you give me what I want – the names of other Thug leaders, help in tracing them down – I'll save you from the gallows. *(Pause.* SLEEMAN *takes out his watch and lays it on the desk in front of* FERINGHEEA*)* You have one minute to make up your mind.

SLEEMAN *walks away and looks out of a window.*

FERINGHEEA: I will tell you.

SLEEMAN: How many murders have you done?

FERINGHEEA: I don't remember.

SLEEMAN: Answer my questions or hang!

FERINGHEEA: I stopped counting, you see. After one thousand.

SLEEMAN: You're proud of it. Don't you feel remorse?

FERINGHEEA: You are big game hunter, Captain Sleeman. Don't you enjoy excitement of stalking animals?

SLEEMAN: We're talking about human beings. First you make friends with them, then you strangle them.

FERINGHEEA: It is higher form of sport than stalking animals. You have only simple instincts of tigers or wild pigs to overcome. We have to lull fears of intelligent men and women. Sometimes carrying weapons, sometimes very well prepared. Once we fell in with Mogul officer, guarded by soldiers, himself well armed. He was highly suspicious, refusing to travel with us. We are persisting. More and more parties of Thugs waiting for him along road and trying to attach themselves to his party. Still he is refusing our company. At last we are arranging a trap. Some pretended sepoys weeping beside their dead comrade at roadside. He cannot then avoid dismounting and praying with them. Mohammedans, you know, cannot pray unless they first lay aside their weapons. So then we are seizing him and the *ruhmal* – this soft cloth, no weapon to compare with his own – is about his neck and grave already prepared for supposed dead man is receiving this proud officer's corpse. You can imagine excitement of chase and successful conclusion. Remorse? Never! Joy and elation! Yes, often!

SLEEMAN: Your methods are not only foul, but cowardly. You never attack until the odds are at least three to one in your favour.

FERINGHEEA: Aren't you surrounding one tiger with many elephants, spears and guns? Even then are you requiring such patience and organisation, such strategy, such playing upon the human heart? I was once in a gang which accompanied sixty men, women and children for two hundred miles before finding the moment to despatch them all. That is big game hunting.

SLEEMAN: How did you become a Thug?

FERINGHEEA: My father gave me the sacred *gur* to eat. Let any man once taste that *gur* and he is Thug for ever. It changes his nature.

SLEEMAN: So it is a kind of religion.

FERINGHEEA: When the world was young the goddess Bhowani did battle with a monster which was threatening to devour mankind. But as fast as Bhowani was killing monster with her sword, its blood was giving birth to new monsters. So, brushing sweat from her own arm, Bhowani created two men. To each she was giving strip of cloth torn from hem of dress, telling them to strangle monsters, but not shed one drop of blood.

SLEEMAN: It makes no difference whether you kill a rich traveller or a poor one?

FERINGHEEA: You are still not understanding. We are killing because we cannot do otherwise. Many of us are highly respectable people – I myself am a Brahmin – but once every year we feel the great urge to steal away from our homes and the places that know us and to go on the roads.

SLEEMAN: Your father first gave you the *gur*. You will give it to your children. The thing is hereditary?

FERINGHEEA: It is very old, very solemn and secret, very enticing profession. You can no more stop Thuggee than you can kill all the tigers in the jungle. But we are not strangling Europeans. Thuggee is doing you no harm, Captain Sleeman. Why are you interfering?

SLEEMAN: I also believe in a God who calls me to do battle with monsters. I wouldn't expect you to understand my other reasons. Pity for the victims and their families. Disinterested justice. Because murder and treachery horrify me.

FERINGHEEA: Because you are hunter. Like me you have eaten *gur*.

SLEEMAN: *(unlocking manacles)* I want names, Feringheea. The name of every Thug you ever knew or heard of and all his sons and grandsons and uncles and cousins.

FERINGHEEA: We are hunting together. I shall be your very best guide, Sleeman Sahib. Now we are truly catching tigers. Nasir, Morlee, Dorgha, Ameer Ali, Buhras Jamadar, Sahib Khan, Rumzam, Dureean . . .

They go out together.

Scene 13. Near Timbuctoo. 1826.

Enter LAING and MOBO, *a young negro*. LAING's *right hand is missing, he has large scars on his face and he walks with a limp. The scene is the inside of a tent. The two are preparing to go to sleep after a day's travelling.*

MOBO: This Sheikh Labeida bad man.

LAING: You have a prejudice against Arabs, Mobo. I'm not surprised, seeing they enslave your race.

MOBO: Very bad man. Worse than Babani.

LAING: I doubt that. Anyway, Babani's dead, you're a free man and we only have to spend a few days more in the company of Sheikh Labeida. Once we meet the regular caravan route our troubles are over.

MOBO: *(points to brooch round LAING's neck)* Sheikh Labeida see that gold bird, like very much.

LAING: This bird is as precious to me as life itself. She put it there with her own hands, my darling Emma. I'll tell you what's worrying me, Mobo. What will she think of me when she sees what I look like now?

MOBO: She go be proud of you, sah. She see you big man.

LAING: Well, we've been to Timbuctoo, you and I, that's the feather in our caps. The pity is, considering what it cost us to get there, that Timbuctoo is such a damned, rotten little place. No streets paved with gold, no rich caravans, no treasure-houses and palaces. Just a jumble of mud huts. A squalid little market-town in the middle of nowhere. We've been to Timbuctoo and wiped it off the map. Will they remember who it was wiped Timbuctoo off the map? Will they, Mobo? Asleep. Lieutenant-Colonel must be the least they can offer me. Emma. Always in my thoughts. But I've completely forgotten your face. *(He kisses the gold brooch)* Not long now. Colonel and Mrs. Laing.

His eyes close and he falls asleep. Enter SHEIKH LABEIDA with a scimitar. He tiptoes across and stands over LAING, then raises scimitar. LAING opens his eyes, half rises, tries to defend himself with his left arm, but is cut down. MOBO leaps up and dodges out. LABEIDA cuts off gold brooch and goes out.

Scene 14. Downing Street. 1831.

Enter LORD GODERICH, meeting LORD PALMERSTON. Both are clutching papers under their arms, on their way to a Cabinet meeting. GODERICH, 49, Secretary of State for the Colonies and once briefly Prime Minister, is an amiable, fussy, irresolute man. PALMERSTON, 47, who has just become Foreign Secretary for the first time, is an elegant, relaxed, commanding one. They were boys at Harrow together.

PALMERSTON: What flusters you today, Goody? The prospect of bloody revolution? Parliament about to be reformed amidst the outcry of the mob? The pillars of old England falling about our ears? We shall pull through. The English are not the French, thank God!

GODERICH: Nothing of any importance. A distant yelp from Tasmania. Do you remember Governor Arthur, Pam?

PALMERSTON: Arthur? Major Arthur, as he then was. A great disciplinarian – he invented a system of flogging by tap of drum. One stroke of the lash and one drum-beat precisely every minute. We sent him off to be Governor of Tasmania, where all the convicts are. He seemed the right man.

GODERICH: Well, now he's exercised on behalf of the Tasmanian aborigines. They're a damned nuisance, but he won't have them exterminated.

PALMERSTON: Gone native?

GODERICH: He decided to round them all up and put them in a reserve. He threw a cordon right across the island, a tremendous operation – the idea being to drive them all into a peninsula with a narrow neck. Unfortunately, not a sausage.

PALMERSTON: What do you mean?

GODERICH: Not one single aborigine entered that blasted peninsula. Poor Arthur's beside himself. He's inundated me with screeds of explanation and apology.

PALMERSTON: He probably wants to be flogged.

GODERICH: No, but seriously, what's to be done?

PALMERSTON: Good Lord! You're not the governor of Tasmania, Goody. Let Arthur worry about what's to be done. You only have to write him a comforting letter saying your faith in his efficiency is in no way impaired, etc. Then in a year or so, if he hasn't made any progress, you can post him off to Canada or wherever.

GODERICH: I suppose so.

PALMERSTON: Now I have a tiresome fellow called Warrington bothering me. His wife is an illicit daughter of our late King and his daughter married a mad Scot who went to Timbuctoo and got his head cut off by Arabs. Warrington thinks the French are at the bottom of it and he broke off diplomatic relations with the Pasha of Tripoli. Well, we've had a frigate making pointed calls on Tripoli for a year or so and the Pasha's eaten humble pie. He's expelled both his chief minister and the French consul, so we've called off the frigate and Warrington's run up his flag again. But he's not by any means satisfied. He wants the minister and the French consul prosecuted. He claims they've stolen all the mad Scot's diaries and papers about his discoveries and they've certainly disappeared. But the French consul has fled to America and the Pasha's minister is skulking in Majorca.

GODERICH: What are you going to do?

PALMERSTON: Nothing. The French have behaved well for once. They've started an inquiry of their own and they've conferred a posthumous gold medal on the mad Scot. The daughter's married a vice-consul and gone to live in Italy. Warrington can go to Timbuctoo himself for all I care.

GODERICH: I sometimes wonder how much we gain by all these distant encumbrances. The Roman Empire was integral to

Roman prosperity, but ours...

PALMERSTON: Perfectly useless. Still, we may not know what we want it all for, but we can be quite certain we don't want others to have it.

GODERICH: The same might be said of the Parliamentary vote.

PALMERSTON: There's only one safe rule for rulers, Goody. Discover what the public wants and lead them loudly and boldly in that direction.

GODERICH: And if the public doesn't know what it wants?

PALMERSTON: Boldly and loudly wait until they've made up their minds.

GODERICH: That's pure democracy.

PALMERSTON: Yes. Though you mustn't let them know it or they'd lose their nerve. Somebody to take responsibility is all they need. But never try to take responsibility for a course of action they don't want.

GODERICH: Nobody wants the Empire.

PALMERSTON: Not yet. They hardly know they've got it. When they find out, they'll all want it.

They go out together.

Scene 15. Kew Gardens. 1856.

Enter HOOKER and BURTON, still in conversation.

HOOKER: I had an interesting day at Mirzapore. I met one of Thuggee Sleeman's assistants and he took me to the gaol to interview a captured specimen. A most amiable chap, this Thug, quite unrepentant and proud to show me the secret of his skill. A knotted cloth round the neck, the knuckles pressed into the spine and hey presto! He reminded me of a hairdresser.

BURTON: You admire Sleeman?

HOOKER: Who doesn't? To root up in ten years an evil which had flourished for centuries! He did it by writing down every Thug's family tree and making copies for his assistants, so that they could hunt them down to the last man. Even their children he took into custody and wouldn't allow them to procreate.

BURTON: Can that be justified?

HOOKER: A gardener wouldn't hesitate to take such action against a deadly parasite.

BURTON: But have the British any right – are they fit – to be the world's gardeners?

HOOKER: These moral questions! I'm a botanist. I'm inclined to believe that God is too.

BURTON: Your father, Mr. Hooker, is the Director of Kew. No doubt you'll succeed him in the post. Suppose that some complete outsider, some non-botanist, came and took your gardens away from you and organised them on some entirely different principle. One which took no account of the life of the plants themselves, their subtleties, their histories, their nature. Wouldn't that seem to you some sort of outrage?

HOOKER: Undoubtedly.

BURTON: That's the outrage the British have committed.

HOOKER: But, Captain Burton, it was you who went to India to conquer. I only went to collect a few rhododenrons.

BURTON: Conquest is nothing. Human history is all conquest and re-conquest. I'm talking about an ideology. It begins from a purely material superiority – advanced weapons, machines, forms of transport – but insinuates itself into the minds of the conquered, so that they come to believe themselves inferior by nature. What follows? A world of slaves dominated by one master-race, materially and morally impregnable, but dead to feeling, dead to thought, dead to spirit.

HOOKER: Our great contribution to human history has been to *free* the slaves.

BURTON: And when will they be free of us, their liberators? Not until the great myth of progress – triumphant materialism – is destroyed.

HOOKER: An alarming view.

BURTON: The British Empire, which thinks of itself as the instrument of Providence for the betterment of mankind, may turn out to be one of the greatest evils that ever threatened the world.

HOOKER: Speaking purely as a botanist, progress isn't a myth. Look at that pretty fellow there, rooted so robustly in foreign soil. The better adapted species inherit the earth, Captain Burton. But speculation about the future of mankind I find rather fruitless. We are too ignorant of ourselves. There is a lady over there by the banana tree who has been observing you discreetly over the page of her book for some time.

BURTON: Good Lord!

HOOKER: You know her?

BURTON: We last met on the ramparts of Boulogne. Six years ago at least. Her mother intervened.

HOOKER: I see no sign of her mother now. When you go looking for the source of the Nile, if you come across any plant that looks interesting, do bring it home with you.

BURTON: Interesting?

HOOKER: Any little living thing.

He goes out.

BURTON: *(as he goes off in the opposite direction)* Miss Arundell? Miss Isabel Arundell?

Scene 16. Trieste. 1884.

ISABEL and BURTON, *in their old age, are seated at the table working on* The Arabian Nights.

OLD BURTON: *(dictating)* 'Then the King arose and did away with his bride's maidenhead.' Got that? Isabel?

OLD ISABEL: Of course I've got it.

OLD BURTON: Read it back to me.

OLD ISABEL: The whole passage?

OLD BURTON: No, just where you've got to. You seemed to be looking out of the window.

OLD ISABEL: The last sentence I took down was the one beginning 'The King arose'. Do you want to stop now, Richard? Are you tired?

OLD BURTON: 'But when it was midnight Shahrazad awoke and signalled to her sister Dunyazad who sat up and said, "Allah upon thee, O my sister, recite to us some new story, delightsome and delectable, wherewith to while away the waking hours of our latter night."' And a footnote.

OLD ISABEL: Yes?

OLD BURTON: 'Latter night' needs explaining to readers ignorant of Arab customs.

OLD ISABEL: The part between the last sleep and dawn.

OLD BURTON: Quite so. 'When they would rise to wash and pray'.

OLD ISABEL: '. . . wash and pray.'

OLD BURTON: Do you remember when all you knew about the East was what was contained in Disraeli's *Tancred*?

OLD ISABEL: I was reading it under the tree in Kew Gardens.

OLD BURTON: You thought it contained the meaning of life.

OLD ISABEL: Did I?

OLD BURTON: You said so at the time.

OLD ISABEL: I really meant that I thought you contained the meaning of life. I hardly needed Disraeli's romance once I had met Richard Burton, did I?

OLD BURTON: And still?

OLD ISABEL: And still.

OLD BURTON: But you don't like mentioning what the King did to his bride's maidenhead.

OLD ISABEL: I think it will offend many of your readers. I don't see that it's necessary.

OLD BURTON: It's what's written in the original. It's the truth of the story. How can you think truth offensive or unnecessary? Truth is the meaning of life. There's no other.

OLD ISABEL: It could be expressed in a different way.

OLD BURTON: It is not expressed in a different way in the Arabic. I am making a faithful translation of *The Arabian Nights*, not telling bedtime stories to children.

OLD ISABEL: Richard, you don't have to justify yourself to me. To the world perhaps, which neither understands nor appreciates you, but never to me.

OLD BURTON: Then why do you take the world's part? The world is afraid of the truth. You and I should never be.

OLD ISABEL: I want the world to love and admire you as I do, not denigrate your name and snigger behind their hands. 'Richard Burton, the great explorer, has now come down in his old age to publishing doubtful books'. That's what they'll say.

OLD BURTON: Isabel, I'm not afraid of what they'll say.

OLD ISABEL: Of course not. But I'm afraid for you. That's my part, has always been my part in all your adventures. Would you have had it otherwise? You never took me with you, did you, on any of your difficult or dangerous expeditions, yet I think you needed me more than if I had been another kind of person.

OLD BURTON: I need you now, just as much as I ever did in Kew Gardens.

OLD ISABEL: I often wonder if you did need me then. I needed you – you were life itself, suddenly tall and strong standing over me. But you – you grew to love me because I loved you.

OLD BURTON: Well, that may be the truth. I never could resist being admired.

OLD ISABEL: If you did ever grow to love me.

OLD BURTON: Shall we give Shahrazad a rest and have some lunch?

OLD ISABEL: Just as you say. I'm afraid it will only be Brand's Essence again for you, my poor darling.

She helps him to his feet and supports him painfully out.

Scene 17. Whitehall. 1839.

PALMERSTON *and his* SECRETARY, *the latter seated at a desk.*

PALMERSTON: 'Secretary of State for Foreign Affairs to the Governor-General of India. My dear Auckland...'

> *Sound of military band in the street outside.* PALMERSTON *goes to the window.*
>
> British troops. Incomparable fellows on the parade-ground. Impossible riff-raff when left to their own devices. But what are they like on the field of battle?

SECRETARY: We know that, my Lord.

PALMERSTON: Do we?

SECRETARY: Waterloo.

PALMERSTON: A quarter of a century ago. These men's fathers fought at Waterloo.

SECRETARY: Burma.

PALMERSTON: That beastly little jungle scrimmage! Fifteen thousand dead of dysentery for the capture of one town. And that was fifteen years ago. Face it, dear boy, we simply don't know what they're like on a field of battle. They've none of them been on one.

SECRETARY: But we're the most powerful nation in the world.

PALMERSTON: Who says so?

SECRETARY: The whole world says so.

PALMERSTON: Why?

SECRETARY: Waterloo.

PALMERSTON: Waterloo.

> *He listens to the band and watches the soldiers until the sound fades away.*

PALMERSTON: It's rickety, dear boy, the whole edifice is rickety. It needs shoring up. 'My dear Auckland . . .' But dammit, a clumsy bit of work could bring the whole thing crashing. Remind me of the salient points.

SECRETARY: Afghanistan and the Punjab. Two neighbouring states hostile to one another, but friendly to us.

PALMERSTON: Equally friendly to us?

SECRETARY: We don't have regular relations with the Afghans, my Lord, but they claim that part of the Punjab belongs to them – the province of Peshawar. If we were to support their claim to Peshawar, the Afghans would certainly be very friendly to us.

PALMERSTON: And if not?

SECRETARY: Russia, on their northern frontier, is making serious overtures.

PALMERSTON: We have a man on the spot?

SECRETARY: Mr. Burnes, 'Bokhara' Burnes, our special envoy in Kabul, speaks highly of the present Afghan ruler, Dost Mohammed, and more or less recommends that we support his claim against the Punjab.

PALMERSTON: But Dost Mohammed is a usurper.

SECRETARY: Of some standing. The legitimate ruler, Shah Shuja, was thrown out some years ago. He was a fairly nasty sort of tyrant – given to blinding people – and Dost Mohammed is a popular ruler.

PALMERSTON: Shah Shuja meanwhile has taken refuge in the Punjab.

SECRETARY: Yes. In the disputed territory – Peshawar.

PALMERSTON: Hm? The Punjab.

SECRETARY: A large and powerful state lying along the northern frontier of British India. Its army is also large and powerful, trained by Europeans and equipped with modern artillery. We are on exceptionally good terms with the Punjab's ruler, the Maharajah Ranjit Singh.

PALMERSTON: What is the immediate cause of the disturbance?

SECRETARY: Shah Shuja wishes to regain his throne in Kabul. He has gathered an army and is about to march. The Maharajah Ranjit Singh supports him, for obvious reasons, but he has also asked for our support.

PALMERSTON: Does he need it?

SECRETARY: Only as a gesture. He wants no more than a few British officers, as military advisers.

PALMERSTON: What is Auckland's view?

SECRETARY: Lord Auckland's special adviser is Sir William Macnaghten, a most experienced political officer and an expert in all Eastern affairs. He is a master of both Hindu and Mohammedan law and his edition of the Arabic text of *The Arabian Nights*, published only last year, is considered by far the most reliable.

PALMERSTON: I wonder if that's relevant.

SECRETARY: Probably not, my Lord. Sir William's political opinion is that this is a major opportunity for us. We should not be content to send military advisers with Shah Shuja's invading force, but should take charge of the whole operation.

PALMERSTON: Send a British army?

SECRETARY: Cement our existing friendship with the Punjab and Maharajah Ranjit Singh. Replace Shah Shuja on his throne, thus putting the legitimate ruler of Afghanistan in our debt. Gain political control over the whole northern frontier area.

PALMERSTON: Macnaghten ignores the villainy of Shah Shuja

and the popularity of Dost Mohammed?

SECRETARY: Sir William disagrees with our man in Kabul, 'Bokhara' Burnes. Sir William distrusts all Afghans and especially the usurper, Dost Mohammed. He is aware of Shah Shuja's personal disadvantages but considers them heavily outweighed by his legitimacy and by the fact that he will owe his throne to us.

PALMERSTON: Thank you. Admirable! That's the local view. Now for the broader one. The map. *(He goes to a map and stabs at it rapidly with his finger)* British India. North of British India, the Punjab. Northwest of the Punjab, Afghanistan. North of Afghanistan . . .

SECRETARY: Russia.

PALMERSTON: Russia. Now an attack from north to south, from Afghanistan on the Punjab, is a blade pointed at our breast. But an attack from the Punjab on Afghanistan?

SECRETARY: A blade pointed at Russia's.

PALMERSTON: Just so. 'My dear Auckland, the British Government gives you full authority to use British troops in order to restore Shah Shuja to the throne of his ancestors . . .' and so forth. Pity Dost Mohammed is such a popular ruler. When we bring this action to the attention of Parliament we shall have to suppress Burnes's favourable comments. The British public wouldn't like us to embroil ourselves in a conflict which was at all ambivalent.

SECRETARY: Would it be a good idea to send Burnes with the army? Since he knows the Afghans and gets on well with them.

PALMERSTON: Excellent! And Macnaghten too, to keep a firm grasp on that rascal Shah Shuja.

SECRETARY: Won't that make it awkward for Burnes, since it's Macnaghten's advice we're taking?

PALMERSTON: Burnes is a loyal servant of the Crown, isn't he?

He'll have to lump it. Give him a knighthood.

They go out.

Scene 18. Tasmania. 1831.

Enter COLONEL ARTHUR *with* GEORGE AUGUSTUS ROBINSON, *a short, stocky Cockney, 43, ex-bricklayer and builder, now non-conformist missionary.*

ARTHUR: Defeat I cannot contemplate, Mr. Robinson. Of course the failure of Operation 'Black Drive' was a bitter blow to me. When the cordon was drawn tight and it became apparent that not one single aborigine had entered the Tasman Peninsula, I was the target for a great deal of abuse and mockery. I do not, on that account, consider that my duty to solve the aborigine problem has been absolved.

ROBINSON: You've prayed for guidance, Colonel Arthur?

ARTHUR: Almighty God must be weary with my prayers. But I don't expect a miracle. This world is almost wholly evil. Men are given up to depravity. The soldiers of Christ are few. Lonely and often discouraged, we struggle through a dark and thorny forest of wickedness and ignorance.

ROBINSON: Things are not as black as that, Colonel Arthur. I believe in miracles. God can clear a path for us if He has a mind to.

ARTHUR: No doubt. But we are not to count on it.

ROBINSON: Well, I count on it. And since you've had the good sense to call me in on this job, you can count on it too. The Almighty has sent me to bring salvation to the aborigines.

ARTHUR: I turn to you, Mr. Robinson, because you have some knowledge of the natives and speak their language. If you should succeed in persuading them to leave the bush, we shall resettle them on one of the islands. I shall then give you the task of supervising the settlement and teaching them the rudiments of Christian living.

ROBINSON: Surely this world is a wonderful place! As Peter the

Fisherman was called from his nets to be a Fisher of men, so I, George Augustus Robinson, was called from laying bricks to lay the foundations of God's new community of Tasmanians. A new life of hope and happiness begins for us all, Colonel Arthur. For you, for me, and for these poor savages.

ARTHUR: Mind you don't get yourself murdered.

ROBINSON: It's not God's will.

They go out.

Scene 19. Hampstead Heath. 1836.

Enter LETTY LANDON *and* GEORGE MACLEAN, *taking a walk. She is 34, a Romantic poetess and novelist, now (1836) less admired than she once was. He is 35, a captain in the African Colonial Corps, now President of the Council of Gold Coast traders.*

LETTY: Eighteen months hard labour! In chains! I'm shocked, Captain Maclean. Adultery isn't a crime in England, why should it be in Africa?

MACLEAN: The chief's justice would have been rougher than mine. Torture followed by execution.

LETTY: I see. You're teaching the natives mercy. But what makes them obey you? You told me the last British Governor of the Gold Coast died at the hands of the Ashantis and they still use his skull as a stirrup-cup. Do you cow them with soldiers?

MACLEAN: I have very few soldiers. A hundred and twenty regulars, including the band.

LETTY: You keep a band in the jungle? That is going a bit far.

MACLEAN: You mustn't think of me as living in a jungle, Miss Landon. Cape Coast Castle is a very respectable building. And the band's a good one. You should hear them play 'Loch Lomond' and 'Over the Sea to Skye'.

LETTY: I wish I could!

MACLEAN: We're a hopelessly masculine society. Traders, soldiers, sailors, the occasional clergyman.

LETTY: Which path shall we take? This one leads up the heath towards the house where Mr. Coleridge lived and this down to Mr. Keats's.

MACLEAN: You choose. Being better read than I am.

LETTY: Oh, I choose Mr. Keats. There never was a poet like him for transporting you into the realms of fancy. Do you ever allow yourself to be transported, Captain Maclean?

MACLEAN: I play my violin.

LETTY: What? In your West African castle? I can hardly wait to hear it.

MACLEAN: You find my life quite comical.

LETTY: Oh, no, I promise you, not comical at all. Very romantic.

MACLEAN: It's not that either. But we have books, you know, in the Castle library. When I said you were better read than me, I didn't mean that I never read any books at all.

LETTY: Captain Maclean, I apologise. You shall have Mr. Keats to take back to Africa with you.

MACLEAN: I'd prefer one of your own books, Miss Landon. If I cannot take their author.

LETTY: Are you inviting me?

MACLEAN: To Cape Coast Castle? Sheer lunacy!

LETTY: If you're asking me, Captain Maclean, I'm coming.

MACLEAN: It's out of the question. If you came, we'd have to be married.

LETTY: Yes, I see no way out of that.

MACLEAN: You mean, no?

LETTY: No, I mean yes.

MACLEAN: I should never have suggested such a thing. The climate's a killer.

LETTY: It hasn't killed you.

MACLEAN: The most dangerous time is the first year.

LETTY: Are you saying now you don't want me?

MACLEAN: On the other hand, the castle's well situated, right over the sea. There's a healthy breeze most of the year.

LETTY: I imagine it blows hot and cold more or less from one minute to the next.

MACLEAN: Forgive me. I had no intention of making such a proposal.

LETTY: But you made it, didn't you?

MACLEAN: I fancy I did.

LETTY: I fancy you did.

MACLEAN: Yes.

LETTY: And now you've thought better of it?

MACLEAN: Miss Landon, what I've said, I've said. Therefore I repeat my proposal, such as it is.

LETTY: Captain Maclean, I accept your proposal, such as it is.

MACLEAN: It's madness. Our friends will tell us so, the world will tell us so. They'll be right. You'll take the next boat home.

LETTY: Don't you think my spirit's at least as strong as yours?

MACLEAN: Stronger.

LETTY: Then let me prove it!

They go out together.

Scene 20. Kabul. 1841.

Enter SIR WILLIAM MACNAGHTEN and SIR ALEXANDER BURNES. MACNAGHTEN is 48, an Ulsterman. He wears spectacles and dresses with extreme formality, up to a top-hat. BURNES is 36, a Scot and distantly related to the poet. He is a famous traveller in the regions north-west of India. He is a soldier who later joined the Indian political service. MACNAGHTEN is a civil administrator. Both men are outstanding linguists.

Sound of military band in the distance.

MACNAGHTEN: Well, Burnes, we can congratulate ourselves. Dost Mohammed the usurper is deposed. Shah Shuja sits securely upon his throne. Kabul is as quiet as an English market-town on a Sunday.

BURNES: I never heard a more dismal sound than those regiments marching away towards the Passes.

MACNAGHTEN: Come on, Burnes, we needed those regiments to restore Shah Shuja, but we shall keep him here by our political arrangements.

BURNES: You mean bribery.

MACNAGHTEN: One gets nowhere in the East without it.

BURNES: Look, Macnaghten, I don't know how much you're paying the hill tribes to keep the Passes open, nor what it's costing to persuade powerful chieftains who normally prefer Dost Mohammed to put up with Shah Shuja, but I'll make a guess that it's more than the government of India can permanently afford. The best part of the army's gone. Let them once clip those subsidies and we're dead men.

MACNAGHTEN: There are four thousand troops remaining in the garrison here for our protection.

BURNES: Camped on an open plain! With ten thousand camp-followers, mostly women and children. They can't protect themselves, let alone us.

MACNAGHTEN: The defences could be better. I'm sure our new general will see to that.

BURNES: Elphinstone? The man's completely past it. The only thing he thinks about is his gout.

MACNAGHTEN: He has a very high reputation. He commanded a battalion at Waterloo. The fact is, Burnes, you will persist in looking on the dark side, because your own advice was overruled. If you want to serve your country, you should think a little less about your personal safety and a little more about how your knowledge and experience can be put to good use.

BURNES: If I had had any thought of personal safety, would I have come back to Kabul?

MACNAGHTEN: It hasn't done your career any harm, Sir Alexander Burnes.

BURNES: My advice to the British Government was not only ignored, everything I said in praise of Dost Mohammed was omitted from the published report. How can any Afghan trust me after that?

MACNAGHTEN: Trust? They don't know the meaning of the word. Their whole way of life is founded on treachery.

BURNES: Oh, it certainly is now. What would you expect when you've installed a puppet ruler by foreign invasion, when you hold him in power with an army of occupation and flagrant bribery?

MACNAGHTEN: Whose side are you on, Burnes?

BURNES: You know whose side I'm on and bloody ashamed of its perversity.

Enter slowly and painfully MAJOR-GENERAL WILLIAM ELPHINSTONE. *He is 59 and crippled with gout.*

ELPHINSTONE: Bickering, gentlemen? This will never do. Think how the safety of so many lives depends on you.

BURNES: Not on us, General Elphinstone. On your army. Yet before the army came here, I was as safe in Kabul as in London.

MACNAGHTEN: Burnes is worried about the defences of the cantonment, General.

ELPHINSTONE: So am I, Sir William. What possessed them to send me here? Done up. Done up in body and mind. However did I get so old? Life's too short. Much too short for bothering arguments.

He hobbles out.

BURNES: Winning Waterloo must have taken a lot out of him.

He and MACNAGHTEN follow ELPHINSTONE out.

Scene 21. Tasmania. 1832.

Enter ROBINSON, with flute. He stands centre and begins to play, all the time watching the edges of the stage. He stops playing and turns slowly round to observe the edges of the forest behind him. He plays again, stops again and turns around, plays again. Then he stops altogether, lowers the flute and waits. After a pause, several ABORIGINES come out of the forest and surround him, pointing their spears at him.

ROBINSON: Don't be afraid. I'm your friend. You can come right up to me. See, no weapons. Nothing but my flute. Come closer. I've something to tell you.

ABORIGINE: You speak our language.

ROBINSON: That's so we can have talking instead of fighting. Will you listen to me?

ABORIGINE: We are listening.

ROBINSON: I can take you to a place where you'll always have food and shelter. Never hungry or cold again. Nobody killing you or taking your women. No more hiding and running.

ABORIGINE: What place?

ROBINSON: Follow me and I'll show you.

ABORIGINE: You take us to the land of the dead? To England?

ROBINSON: England? No, no. I won't take you to England.

ABORIGINE: We want to go to England.

ROBINSON: England's full of white men. Do you like white men?

ABORIGINE: We don't like white men, but they're very powerful. We want to be white men.

ROBINSON: Going to England won't turn you into white men.

ABORIGINE: We die and go to the land of the dead. Then we become powerful spirits like other white men.

ROBINSON: England is just a place on earth like this place. White men are just ordinary men like you. When white men die they go to a place called Heaven. Up there. Beautiful climate. Singing and dancing all day. Some white men go there. Bad white men go to another place called Hell. Down there. Terribly hot. Groaning and crying all day. Heaven is not kept just for white men. I can show you how to go there, if you follow me.

ABORIGINE: You have food?

ROBINSON: Plenty of food. And white men's clothes. This very night you can all have a great feast at my camp.

ABORIGINE: We are coming with you.

ROBINSON: You won't regret it. Now let's go and fetch the rest of your people.

ABORIGINE: Yes. Good. You give us a feast and then take us to Heaven-England.

ABORIGINES break into an excited dance, with whoops and cries, then run out.

ROBINSON: Lord, this is a good start. Thank you.

He goes out after them.

Scene 22. Kabul. 1841.

GENERAL ELPHINSTONE *wrapped in rugs and lying on a* chaise-longue. MACNAGHTEN *standing over him.*

MACNAGHTEN: General Elphinstone, you've got to send troops into the city. Kabul is in uproar. Crowds are roaming the streets.

ELPHINSTONE: We had such a peaceful summer. Pony-racing and theatricals, parties and polo. I was beginning to think they'd pensioned me off to the right spot. Now the weather's turned nasty and so have the natives.

MACNAGHTEN: I demand action.

ELPHINSTONE: Demands! Demands! They can't necessarily be met. Disturbances in Nijrow, disturbances in Kohistan, unrest in the Passes . . . I'm not prepared to disperse all the troops.

MACNAGHTEN: What the devil are your troops for if not to keep the peace in Kabul?

ELPHINSTONE: I'm only a plain soldier, Macnaghten, and I never did understand politics, but surely disturbances of this kind do not occur in a well-run country?

MACNAGHTEN: Afghanistan is hardly a country. It's a jigsaw of different factions. The Government of India has been subsidising several of these factions and can no longer afford to do so at the rate of one-and-a-quarter million pounds per annum. These disturbances are caused by a cut in the subsidies. They are a try-on. We have only to make a show of our superior strength and they will die away immediately.

ELPHINSTONE: Dear me! But we don't have superior strength. You'll have to apply to the Government of India, Macnaghten, not to me.

Enter DOCTOR BRYDON, *hot and dishevelled. He salutes.*

BRYDON: General Elphinstone, sir . . .

ELPHINSTONE: Ah, Doctor Brydon. I was in some pain this morning, doctor, but for some reason it's eased off a little.

BRYDON: Burnes has been murdered.

ELPHINSTONE: Murdered?

MACNAGHTEN: Sir Alexander Burnes?

BRYDON: The mob surrounded his house and dragged him out. He was hacked to pieces.

ELPHINSTONE: My God! Poor fellow!

MACNAGHTEN: I warned him not to stay in the city. So much for trusting Afghans! General Elphinstone, you must send troops into Kabul this instant.

BRYDON: The riot is quite out of hand, sir.

MACNAGHTEN: General, will you do as I ask?

ELPHINSTONE: I'm trying to get time to think. Time to collect my elderly wits.

MACNAGHTEN: We shall none of us leave Afghanistan alive. Do you need time to get that into your thick head?

ELPHINSTONE: Fetch me another cushion, Brydon! The pain's coming back.

> *Enter CAPTAIN TREVOR, Macnaghten's intelligence officer. He salutes.*

TREVOR: Sir William!

MACNAGHTEN: Captain Trevor, you've heard the news?

TREVOR: *(taking him aside)* I have a message from Dost Mohammed's son.

MACNAGHTEN: Akbar Khan? This riot is his doing.

TREVOR: He's willing to call it off and calm the city. On condition that you sign an agreement with him. The terms are a bit tricky. You must renounce your previous agreements with other chiefs and make Akbar Khan Prime Minister. In return Shah Shuja will be allowed to keep his throne and the British to remain in Kabul. Otherwise Akbar Khan will make common cause with the other chiefs, close the Passes and starve us out.

MACNAGHTEN: Tricky? Everyone is to lose except Akbar Khan.

TREVOR: And us, sir. We gain a good deal if Akbar Khan really is powerful enough to govern the country.

MACNAGHTEN: But he's Dost Mohammed's son. Why is he offering to keep Shuja on the throne?

TREVOR: Just selling his father, sir, to secure his own advancement. Normal Afghan practice, surely?

MACNAGHTEN: General Elphinstone, for the last time, will you send troops into Kabul?

ELPHINSTONE: No, Macnaghten. No, I won't.

MACNAGHTEN: You're saying that in spite of the troops we're powerless against a mob?

ELPHINSTONE: *Because of* the troops and their women and children. We are responsible for too many lives. God knows, to die oneself would be no hardship.

MACNAGHTEN: In your case, I imagine it would be a welcome release. *(aside to TREVOR)* Where am I to meet Akbar Khan?

TREVOR: He'll send you the agreement to sign tonight and he'll meet you tomorrow morning on the plain between the cantonment and the city.

MACNAGHTEN: In the snow?

TREVOR: So it seems.

MACNAGHTEN: Tell him I'll be there.

> TREVOR *salutes and goes out.* ELPHINSTONE, *helped by* BRYDON, *gets to his feet.*

ELPHINSTONE: This is a bad business. Burnes is a sad loss. For God's sake, let's have some lunch. It may be our last.

> *He hobbles out.* BRYDON *and* MACNAGHTEN *follow.*

Scene 23. Zululand. 1835.

DINGAAN, *Shaka's half-brother, murderer and successor, is seated in the European armchair presented to Shaka in a previous scene. DINGAAN is middle-aged, grossly fat, the Zulu version of a Roman Emperor. Beside him stands JAKOT.*

JAKOT: Many years ago, King Dingaan, the white traders gave this chair to your brother Shaka. In return he gave them land. I told him then that if he gave land to traders, missionaries would come after them. He took no notice. Now here is the first missionary. Send him away.

DINGAAN: I want to see him.

> JAKOT *shrugs and makes a signal. Enter COMMANDER ALLEN FRANCIS GARDINER, RN, aged 41, dressed in his best naval uniform. He salutes DINGAAN.*

DINGAAN: This is no missionary, but a king.

JAKOT: *(crossing to GARDINER)* King Dingaan takes you for a king.

GARDINER: Nothing of that sort, I'm afraid. No more than a sailor who has left the service of his earthly king at sea the better to serve his Heavenly King on land. I'm glad King Dingaan likes my uniform. I wore it especially to do him honour.

JAKOT: *(returning to DINGAAN)* A missionary, as I thought. He's wearing the uniform to impress you.

DINGAAN: Ask him to show me the back.

JAKOT *(to GARDINER)* Please turn around.

GARDINER: Of course. *(he does so)*

DINGAAN: Wonderful clothes!

JAKOT: I'll tell him to go now.

DINGAAN: Not yet. Make complaints about the traders.

JAKOT: *(crossing to GARDINER)* King Dingaan is angry with the traders at Port Natal. They stir up troubles among his subjects, they give refuge to his enemies. This must stop or he will take away their land.

GARDINER: I also disapprove of the traders. Their relations with the local women, for example, are deplorable. But this question of giving refuge to Dingaan's enemies . . . it's said that he murdered his own brother, Shaka . . . we've also heard that he had several of his own wives cut into little pieces because they annoyed him their with chatter. We can't turn people over to Dingaan for this kind of treatment.

JAKOT: If the traders take Dingaan's land, they must keep their treaties with him. *(He returns to DINGAAN and confers with him)* Dingaan will forgive the traders' past offences, provided they keep their word in future. But he doubts if they will keep their word.

GARDINER: He shouldn't doubt it. No true Englishman ever breaks a treaty. It's a matter of honour with us always to keep our word. If he's come across people who've said one thing and done another, then he's been unlucky. They cannot have been the right sort of Englishmen.

JAKOT confers with DINGAAN, who suddenly points at GARDINER.

JAKOT: Dingaan is satisfied. He says that he's now dealing with a king and if he has the king's word, there's nothing more to worry about.

GARDINER: I am not a king, as I explained, but I think I am the right sort of Englishman.

JAKOT confers with DINGAAN.

JAKOT: What do you want from King Dingaan?

GARDINER: Only a little land. To build a church. And to be

allowed to spread the word of God among his people.

JAKOT confers with DINGAAN

JAKOT: Dingaan grants you the land and says you can speak to his people if they want to hear you.

GARDINER: He is a truly magnanimous king. I'm sure that all the stories I've heard are malicious fabrications.

JAKOT: In return, you must do something for Dingaan.

GARDINER: With the greatest pleasure.

JAKOT: There are two women, wives of his chieftains, who have behaved wickedly and broken the law. They took lovers. Now they've escaped to Port Natal with their servants and three children. These women, their servants and their children must be brought before King Dingaan to decide if they are innocent or guilty.

GARDINER: But this is no task for a man of God. Our Lord was especially forgiving to the woman taken in adultery.

JAKOT: Otherwise no land, no speaking to Dingaan's people.

GARDINER: Then I see that in God's service I must do it. But only on the understanding that Dingaan will treat the women justly and mercifully.

JAKOT confers with DINGAAN, who rises ponderously, advances towards GARDINER and suddenly throws his arms round him.

JAKOT: The King of the Zulus embraces a true Englishman.

GARDINER, released, bows and goes out.

JAKOT: The man's a fool. We've nothing to fear from him.

DINGAAN: Wonderful clothes!

They go out laughing.

Scene 24. Cape Coast Castle. 1838.

LETTY LANDON seated at a small desk, writing a letter. Distant sound of breakers and unaccompanied violin off. LETTY stops writing and listens to violin, then she picks up the letter and reads through it quickly in an undertone.

LETTY: 'Dearest Maria, I continue to play Robinson Crusoe. I continue to hear the Atlantic breakers beating far below on the bastions of our castle. Captain Maclean continues to work all day and much of the night and to play his violin of an evening. It is as if we were marooned out of time, out of place, here in our faery castle perched on the edge of a dark land, where the only light is that of Captain Maclean's justice . . .'

She throws down the letter on the desk and walks about.

If only I could talk to you, Maria. I sound unhappy, but I'm not. Things are better than I expected. We're not troubled by heat, or insects. And I must tell you, my husband is a great man. Of course I saw him as that when I first met him and loved him for the dangers he had passed, but now I'm sure of it. His position here is so strange. He has no right, no legal right, to give justice to the negroes. It's they who come and ask for it. "The white man in whose time all men sleep sound". That's what the Ashantis call him. Day after day they come to the Castle; these savages, bringing their debtors, adulterers, robbers, murderers for him to punish or release. How he listens to them! What patience and care! He finds it hard to make up his mind. But once given, his judgment is as that of the Medes and Persians. Oh, he is a man, Maria, to whom the noble Othello was but a poor soldier. My Captain Maclean is soldier, statesman, judge, father counsellor, yes, and even a kind of saint. Not that he's religious in the tiresome way, but secretly, surely, indefatigably, he is led by some vision. Of what? I believe he means to leave here, or more likely die here, having turned a wild confusion of the primitive into the first draft of a civilization.

She sits down. The violin starts another tune.

But I? Why am I here? What am I doing to further this great work? True, I've presided over a few dinner-parties for this or that trader or visiting sea-captain from the anti-slavery patrol. I'm a curiosity. The mad poetess from London. They none of them believe I can stay. One of them bet me I'd take the next boat home. Well, it sailed this morning, Maria, and on it went our steward's wife, who has been my only real friend here, but on it did not go I.

She gets up and walks about.

Here I am still in my lady's chamber, with its black-and-white tiled floor and its beautiful blue walls and its prints of scenes from Shakespeare and the breakers dashing below and the palms waving on the white shore and Captain Maclean playing the violin and all the romance of Africa at my back. It is romantic, isn't it, to think that here alone we stand, like Othello and Desdemona against the Turk, giving laws to our black Cypriots? And not even an Iago to poison our idyll.

She goes to the desk.

Do I sound unhappy, Maria? No, I don't regret that busy, gossipy, back-biting literary life we were all caught up in. I couldn't go back to it now. No, he is kindness itself, when we meet for supper. He doesn't love me, but he didn't when we married. He repented his proposal almost at once, but in all things his word is his bond. I held him to it for a less noble reason, because I was restless and growing old, and saw no other outcome but suicide. Not love, though, not love on either side.

She listens to the violin.

But I'm kind to him too. Oh, we're amazed to see one another so mutually kind, day by day, at breakfast and at supper, and we've nursed each other through sickness with more than kindness, almost with love. He is my admiration and I am his curiosity, set down here like the black-and-white tiles or the Shakespeare prints to remind him of civilization in case he should ever lose sight of it amongst the savagery he does battle with. But knight errants and their ladies shouldn't be regularly at home together.

She picks up the letter.

Why then didn't I sail away? Because England from here does not appear real. The reality is those vile chiefs with their grins and their necklaces of bones and their barking babble and their slaves and their wives and their blood, blood, blood. Oh, you'd hardly guess in London that we're all made of blood. But here we're nothing else. This is what it is to be human, dearest Maria, this pinched, burdened, squalid, dirty, hot, stinking existence in mud and dust, this slavery to superstition, stupidity, greed, cruelty and purposelessness. Civilization is only the veil. Captain Maclean is not such a great man, now I come to think of it. He's wasting his life and his energy. It will come to nothing and no one will ever care.

She goes to window, opens it, crumples letter and throws it out.

Sea! Desolation! I'm utterly wrong. If I could only talk to you, Maria, you'd tell me I was wrong and make me believe it. Two of your novels are in Captain Maclean's library – such a friendly sight. But books won't do here. Just curiosities. Yes, I should have taken the boat. You wouldn't have complained, would you, Captain Maclean, if I'd deserted you? You expected me to, you urged me to. And you won't complain, will you? You'll bow your head once, tears will start in your eyes, and you'll soldier on – England and St. George! You good, great man. You cruel, unloving stranger in a desert of horror, boredom, death.

She picks up a phial and swallows the contents.

I donate my skull to the Ashantis!

She goes hurriedly out, stumbling slightly.

Scene 25. Kabul. 1841.

AKBAR KHAN *seated on a carpet on the ground. A crowd of Afghan warriors and chieftains behind. In front of* AKBAR KHAN *is a pair of handsome pistols in a box with the lid open. Enter* MACNAGHTEN, *dressed in black with a top-hat, followed by* CAPTAIN TREVOR.

MACNAGHTEN: Akbar Khan?

AKBAR KHAN: Sir William Macnaghten. Be seated, please.

> MACNAGHTEN *sits on carpet facing* AKBAR KHAN. TREVOR *stands at the side.*
>
> Christmas weather, isn't it?

MACNAGHTEN: Very seasonable. But in England it would never occur to us to lay a carpet on the snow and hold a meeting out of doors.

AKBAR KHAN: It is always best to do things in the open and we shall not take long. I must first thank you, Sir William, for this handsome present of pistols.

MACNAGHTEN: Captain Trevor suggested you would appreciate them.

AKBAR KHAN: I am quite delighted. Also by the document with your signature delivered to me last night by Captain Trevor. Are you ready, Sir William, to put into effect the proposals contained in this document?

MACNAGHTEN: Perfectly ready.

AKBAR KHAN: You renounce all previous agreements with the chiefs Zeman Khan and Amenoollah Khan and you appoint me, Akbar Khan, Prime Minister to Shah Shuja?

MACNAGHTEN: Quite so.

AKBAR KHAN: In return Shah Shuja is to keep his throne and

the British Army is to remain in Kabul?

MACNAGHTEN: That is the agreement I have signed.

AKBAR KHAN: And which, on your honour as an Englishman, you mean to keep?

MACNAGHTEN: Why not?

> AKBAR KHAN *makes a signal and the Afghans surround* MACNAGHTEN *and* TREVOR.

AKBAR KHAN: Why not, Sir William? Because it is treachery. Look, here are Zeman Khan and Amenoollah Khan in person. When I showed them the signed document they would not believe an Englishman capable of such a thing. Now you have told them with your own lips how you mean to betray them. You don't say a word, Sir William. You have not a word to say.

MACNAGHTEN: The treachery was yours, Akbar Khan.

AKBAR KHAN: Not at all. Mine was pretended treachery, to bait a trap. But it was you that fell into the trap and lost your honour for ever. Seize them!

> TREVOR *is seized from behind.* MACNAGHTEN *makes a lunge towards* AKBAR KHAN.

MACNAGHTEN: You devil!

> AKBAR KHAN *grabs* MACNAGHTEN *by both arms and pins him down.*

AKBAR KHAN: Ah, don't try to fight with me. I am a younger and stronger man. And now you've lost your top-hat, Sir William, as well as your honour.

MACNAGHTEN: Take your hands off me! I am Her Majesty's Envoy. You will be punished for this, Akbar Khan.

AKBAR KHAN: Take him by the legs!

> *Afghans seize* MACNAGHTEN's *legs.*

Drag the traitor to Kabul!

They begin to drag him out.

MACNAGHTEN: For God's sake!

AKBAR KHAN: You call on God! This is how God punishes faithless men!

He picks up the two pistols and fires at MACNAGHTEN as they all rush out, dragging the two Englishmen.

Scene 26. Flinders Island, Tasmania. 1838.

ROBINSON *at a lectern.*

ROBINSON: Once more we are gathered to mourn. Our brothers and sisters, Washington, Romeo, Hannibal, Achilles, Ismene and Antigone, have gone to be with God in Heaven. I know how sad you are. Since I became your Superintendent, our lives have been shared in everything. But why do so many of us die? Do you think it was a mistake to leave the places you know and to follow me and my flute to this island? Trust me, God has a purpose for you. When you roamed over the whole of Tasmania, you were heathens, you did not know God. When I brought you out of the bush, there were no more than one hundred and fifty of you left in the whole of Tasmania; miserable, starved, living like hunted animals. Now, it's true, you are reduced to eighty. But there is a difference! Then you knew only of creation, now you know of salvation. Then, you died and your soul was lost. Now when you die, God sends his angel spirits to lift your soul to Heaven, where there is no sickness, no cold, no hunger, but everlasting happiness.

Pause

Why then are you still unhappy on earth? Because you have not yet accepted that this earth is the preparation for Heaven. You have not cast off your former ways of life. Listen! We give you good, warm clothes. What do you do but sell them to the whalers? Or lose them, or tear them. Listen! We give you houses with wooden floors and stone walls, with cupboards and beds and tables, such as you never knew before. What do you do to them? Damage them, fail to care for them, move fecklessly from one house to another. You have a complete disregard for the valuable property bestowed on you. When I ask you to dig, cut down trees, build the road down to the beach, you complain and shirk and do the work badly. You are lazy and unreliable. But all this work is for your own convenience and improvement, for your own good. Christians are civilized people. You cannot go to Heaven unless you are hard-working and careful. As you have put off the grease which once covered your bodies, so you must put off all your heathen ways. In mourning for our dead brothers and sisters, let us all resolve to take a new grip on our own lives.

Pause

Dear friends, I have another sad thing to say. I have been called to a new task, to be Chief Protector of the Aborigines in New South Wales, across the sea in Australia. I am not to be with you here any longer. But you will not be left comfortless. Mr. Denison will take my place and continue to lead you in the ways I have shown you. You know that I shall never forget you or regret that it was given to me to bring you to Salvation.

He plays his flute.

May God protect you and keep you, my beloved Tasmanians.

He goes out.

Scene 27. Zululand. 1835.

DINGAAN *is sitting on his throne, with* JAKOT *standing beside him. Enter* GARDINER, *in full naval uniform as before.*

GARDINER: I'm here to ask King Dingaan to show compassion.

JAKOT: Dingaan is delighted to see your uniform again.

GARDINER: I feel a special responsibility for the fate of these women, since it was I who returned them to the King for justice.

JAKOT: The king thinks it must be a soldier's uniform.

GARDINER: No. A sailor's.

JAKOT: Is it for fighting?

GARDINER: It's for wearing on special occasions like this. I put it on to signify that, although I am a man of God, I am also an Englishman who once fought for my King against the tyrant Napoleon Bonaparte. An Englishman is always ready to fight injustice and tyranny.

JAKOT confers with DINGAAN.

JAKOT: Dingaan thinks it very unsuitable for fighting. His own warriors fight naked.

GARDINER: I am asking King Dingaan, for the sake of our treaty and friendship, to spare these women's lives.

JAKOT confers with DINGAAN.

JAKOT: Dingaan is sorry to hear this. He thought you were a man of your word. Now you want to break the treaty. You're like all other white men.

GARDINER: I don't want to break the treaty. It's because I've kept my word against my conscience that these women are to die.

JAKOT: Not at all. It's because these women took lovers that they are to die. Nothing to do with you.

GARDINER: Surely he can show mercy?

JAKOT confers with DINGAAN.

JAKOT: Dingaan wishes to know why you wear such a fine uniform when you're only a missionary.

GARDINER: I've already explained that.

JAKOT: He's wondering if you really are a missionary, or perhaps after all a soldier.

GARDINER: I am not a soldier. This is a sailor's uniform.

JAKOT: He doesn't understand the difference. He has no sailors in his army.

GARDINER: Will he or will he not consider my request?

JAKOT confers with DINGAAN.

JAKOT: Dingaan wonders if you understand what a powerful king he is.

GARDINER: Certainly. None more powerful in all this part of Africa.

JAKOT confers with DINGAAN.

JAKOT: His Majesty wishes you to make your request again. Kneeling before him.

GARDINER: Kneeling? That I cannot do. I wear my own King's uniform. He would not permit me to kneel to anyone except himself or God.

JAKOT confers with DINGAAN.

JAKOT: He will kill the women unless you kneel.

GARDINER: Then they must die.

JAKOT confers with DINGAAN.

JAKOT: He says that you can take off your king's uniform and kneel.

GARDINER: That's asking too much.

JAKOT: You're asking too much. Dingaan has given you land and permission to spread your witchcraft in return for these women. Why should he spare them?

GARDINER: I will do it. Our Lord Jesus Christ suffered worse humiliation than this to redeem mankind.

He takes off his uniform and lays it carefully on the ground. JAKOT and DINGAAN watch closely, smiling and making comments to each other.

GARDINER: I kneel before you, King Dingaan, not as a representative of my King and Nation, but as a humble follower of Christ. In His Name I ask you to show mercy to the women.

JAKOT: King Dingaan grants your request. He will not kill the women.

GARDINER: God be praised! I thank you, King Dingaan, from the bottom of my heart.

He stands up. DINGAAN beams.

JAKOT: The women will be punished, of course. But Dingaan will not kill them.

GARDINER: That's all I ask. Please tell him how grateful I am.

He starts to put on his uniform.

JAKOT: They will be tightly bound with ropes.

GARDINER: I don't want to know the details. I accept that they have to be punished in some way.

JAKOT: They will be given no food or water.

GARDINER: What do you mean? For how long?

JAKOT: *(shrugs)*

GARDINER: Do you mean they'll starve?

JAKOT: Maybe. Maybe the ropes will kill them first.

GARDINER: Inhuman! This is worse than execution. Better kill them outright.

JAKOT: Dingaan has promised not to kill them.

GARDINER: He promised mercy!

    JAKOT confers with DINGAAN.

JAKOT: No, he didn't promise mercy.

GARDINER: I protest! I violently protest! He promised mercy by implication.

JAKOT: King Dingaan has finished listening. You are please to leave the kraal now and keep treaties without complaints. In particular you are please to find the children and servants of these women and send them also to King Dingaan. Otherwise he will consider the treaty broken. Your church will be demolished and you will have to return to England.

GARDINER: Monstrous! Monstrous injustice!

    DINGAAN rises with difficulty and goes out.

This is your doing, I suppose. Revenge for the wrongs you suppose you've suffered. Revenge at the expense of two unhappy creatures of your own race.

JAKOT: If I were King of the Zulus, I should not kill these women, but send the *impis* to drive you and traders and all white men into the sea. Dingaan is a fool. Don't forget to send the children and servants.

He goes out.

GARDINER: Almighty God! *(He kneels)* Which way to serve you? To save lives or souls? Don't leave the choice to me. No, you've not left me the choice. What are lives compared to immortal souls? My mission must continue.

He gets up and goes out.

Scene 28. Jalalabad. 1842.

Thick snow. Enter DOCTOR BRYDON *in a tattered great-coat, his head bare except for a rough bandage, his left hand covered in clotted blood, one of his boots missing and replaced with a dirty piece of cloth, limping from a wound in the left knee. He is unarmed.*

BRYDON: What happened to Sir William Macnaghten? No, that was long ago, before the surrender, before we left Kabul. Somebody saw his head on a pole. What happened to General Elphinstone? He was still with us at the Loghur River. Yes, and in the Khoord Kabul Pass where he gave up the wounded and the married officers and their families to Akbar Khan. Yes, and at Kutta Sing, after they'd been firing down at us from the heights all day. Yes, and at Jugdulluk. But at Jugdulluk he went to Akbar Khan to treat for safe conduct and never returned. At Jugdulluk I lost my boot. Also my cap and my horse. But I got another horse from a Hindustani saddler who was shot to blazes and fell down the cliff taking one stirrup with him. Bad luck it was the wrong stirrup, the boot-side stirrup, my bare foot felt as if it was on fire against the cold iron. And there I met Brigadier Anguetil. What happened to him? Asked me how they were doing in the rear. I said they were being cut up in great numbers and he rode back to see. That's what happened to Brigadier Anguetil. Then Captain Bellew took command and we got to Gundumuck. What happened to Captain Bellew? We came to a fork, one road up through the hills, the other down into the valley. Mr. Bailiss said the valley was safest, I said the hills. That's what happened to Bailiss and his party. Our party got in sight of Futtehabad and Captain Bellew went into the village for bread. That's what happened to Captain Bellew. Then the villagers and some Afghan cavalry came after us. Captain Hopkins, Captain Collyer and Dr. Harper were well mounted and they got away. Lieutenant Steer and myself were the only ones left behind them. Lieutenant Steer's horse was done up and so was he. He said he'd hide in a cave. That's what happened to Lieutenant Steer. So I was alone, with Hopkins, Collyer and Harper somewhere in front of me. What happened to me? Twenty men blocking the road in front, picking up large stones to throw. Got the pony to a gallop and passed right through them cutting right and left with my sword. Then another party the same, but a man on a mound with a gun. His shot broke my sword six inches from the hilt and wounded the pony in the loins. But I got clear and met five horsemen leading off three spare horses. That's what happened to Hopkins, Collyer and Harper. Then one of the horsemen came after me and cut at my head with his sword, while I guarded with my six-inch blade and was left with only the hilt. Then he made another cut and I threw the hilt at his head and swerving to avoid it he cut me over the hand. Then I stretched down to reach for the bridle and he thought I had a pistol and made off. And then my pony lay down under me and this is what's happened to me.

He stops and looks up.

A fortress. I'm standing under the walls of Jalalabad and that's the Union Jack.

He waves feebly and begins to move slowly on. Enter CAPTAINS SINCLAIR and CUNNINGHAM.

SINCLAIR: Are you the messenger?

BRYDON: Doctor Brydon, attached to the Sixth Regiment of Shah Shuja's force.

SINCLAIR: Are you the messenger, Brydon?

BRYDON: Messenger?

CUNNINGHAM: We've been expecting a messenger from General Elphinstone's Kabul Army.

BRYDON: Yes, I believe I am. I believe I'm all that remains of General Elphinstone's Kabul Army.

They take him by the arms and help him out.

Scene 29. Kew Gardens. 1856.

BURTON *is sitting down, copying a poem. ISABEL enters and watches him. When he has finished, he looks up, sees and joins her. He hands her the poem.*

BURTON: For you, Isabel. No, don't read it now. Something to keep.

ISABEL: You're going to Africa. When?

BURTON: I hate partings. I'll slip away between one day and the next.

ISABEL: You'll never come back. These last two weeks will turn into a dream, something I won't believe happened.

She suddenly kneels in front of him and clasps his knees.

I have no shame. One should kneel only to God, but I don't want you to go and I've nothing to make you stay except a kind of worship. I know it's not done to show somebody that they're far above you, but what's that to a whole life lost?

BURTON: I shall have to come back to you, Isabel, if only because you're somebody I can talk to. I mean really talk to, not monkey-talk. When I was in India and got tired of that kind of chatter in the Mess, I took myself off to my own quarters and settled down with forty monkeys. I found their language consisted of about sixty words, which was probably as many as were ever used in the Mess.

ISABEL: What about the man who's going with you?

BURTON: Speke? We haven't much in common. For me exploring is a kind of learning. Speke has no curiosity. Partly he enjoys the freedom – being out in the open. Partly it's the sport – what he can shoot. Partly it's a perpetual test of his own virility. I've noticed a peculiar habit of his. When he's succeeded in shooting a pregnant animal, he likes to eat the embryo.

ISABEL: Couldn't anything make you change your mind? If I told you I was afraid of what might happen? A sort of presentiment.

BURTON: I long ago made up my mind that fear is really the worst thing in life. Because it stands in the way of life. Stops you looking at what's really there, stops you doing what you want to do. Intellectual fear and physical fear, both killers. If you can master both, the whole world is open to you, its mysteries and its pleasures.

ISABEL: You're only looking for a river.

BURTON: A river with a name.

ISABEL: Because it will give you a name? You already have one.

BURTON: I like admiration. I like success. But it's not quite that. Success, in any case, is a melancholy thing. You ride for weeks and months in its shadow, but when you reach it, it's a wraith, smoke, without substance. What I want is to be, however briefly and marginally, unique, indispensable. If it weren't for a few particular people we'd still be living in caves. What most people call civilization is only respectability and boredom. The real civilization has to be earned and fought for at every moment of history. It's the life of the mind and the will. Of all the best minds and the bravest wills down the centuries. Nothing lasts but that. In the Indian jungle you find colonies of monkeys living in abandoned towns, among ruined temples and pavements with the grass growing through. That's the civilization our monkey-people are proud of, things they couldn't make themselves and don't understand the meaning of. But somewhere else, the few, the best, are clearing a new field and making a new town.

ISABEL: I know you don't believe in God, not in the way I do. But will you wear this? We Catholics call it 'the miraculous medal'.

BURTON: *(taking it)* The Virgin Mother. *(hands it back)*

ISABEL: You won't wear it?

BURTON: Not on that gold chain. They'll cut my throat for it out there.

ISABEL: Couldn't you ever bear to live in England? To put up with 'civilisation'?

BURTON: Could you bear to give it up? You'd have to leave everything behind – friends, family. I believe you could. When I come back from Africa, will you marry me? Don't answer now. Think it over.

Pause.

Forgive me. I oughtn't to have asked so much.

ISABEL: I've been thinking it over for six years – since I first saw you at Boulogne. I've prayed for you every morning and night. I'd rather have a crust and a tent with you than be Queen of all the world. Yes, yes, yes.

They embrace, rather chastely and hesitantly.

BURTON: At Boulogne? You expected us to meet again.

ISABEL: I knew it. It was our destiny.

BURTON: Hidden from me.

ISABEL: You were looking in another direction.

BURTON: It's true I rather fancied my cousin at the time.

ISABEL: No, another lady. The one you've written this poem to. Fame.

BURTON: You make me sound promiscuous.

ISABEL: I'm not jealous. I know she's your mistress. But I shall be your wife. And you'll come home to me. Always and always. My earthly master!

She takes his hand and leads him out.

Scene 30. Tasmania. 1848.

ROBERT CLARK, Superintendent of the Aborigines, and Mrs CLARK are sitting drinking tea with five ABORIGINES, who wear Scotch bonnets.

MRS. CLARK: Would anyone like another cup of tea?

CLARK: I can recommend these buns.

MRS. CLARK: Sugar and milk?

CLARK: What did I tell you, dear friends? When you left Flinders Island you were in despair. Mr. Robinson gone to Australia, Mr. Denison worn down with worry. Only forty-four of you surviving. And here at Oyster Cove our new quarters didn't look very welcoming. A barrack built by convicts, marshes and mud-flats stretching to the edge of the grey sea. But I reminded you of Adam and Eve, how when they were driven out of Paradise the world must have looked equally sad and inhospitable to them. So we all set to work, just as they must have done, digging and sowing, cleaning and refreshing, building and repairing. Milk? It's from our own cows, remember. And the butter is ours too, from our own dairy – thanks to Mrs Clark here – and for supper we shall eat our own beans and peas and potatoes. All this we've accomplished already, besides turning our hands to any number of useful crafts; weaving and spinning, basket-making and wood-carving. Which of you does not give thanks to God for His great goodness? God never meant you to be anything but happy. He made this world a garden for us, that Adam and Eve and all their children should multiply and populate the earth and enjoy its fruits.

ABORIGINE: We are not having children any more.

CLARK: Not at present. We must see that as part of God's purpose.

ABORIGINE: It is a punishment for our wickedness.

CLARK: Oh, no, no. You were not wicked, only ignorant. When

God is ready He will give you the blessing of children. Trust in Him. Now, we mustn't sit wasting time and thinking idle thoughts. Back to work! The sooner we can drain that next bit of marsh, the sooner we can plant our next crop.

ABORIGINE: God is waiting too long. We are getting old.

CLARK: Old? Nonsense. You're in the prime of life.

ABORIGINES are going out.

MRS CLARK: *(in low voice)* How could you say that, Robert?

CLARK: Say what?

MRS CLARK: Haven't you noticed? Every one of their women is past childbearing age. God will have to work a miracle if He wants to save the Tasmanian aborigines.

They go out after the ABORIGINES.

Scene 31. Lucknow. 1857.

ENTER SUBAHDAR, *marching stiffly. He halts, does an about turn and addresses assembled regiments in the wings.*

SUBAHDAR: Parade! 'Shun!

>*Sound of regiments coming to attention.*
>
>Present arms!
>
>*Sound of drill movement and bugle.*
>
>Order arms!
>
>*Sound of rifles brought to side. Enter SIR HENRY LAWRENCE, 51, Chief Commissioner of Oudh, a gaunt man with a brusque manner.*

LAWRENCE: Thank you, Subahdar. Stand easy, please.

SUBAHDAR: Chief Commissioner of Oudh, Sir Henry Lawrence, will now address you. Parade! Stand at ease!

>*Sound of drill movement. SUBAHDAR marches to one side, halts and stands at ease, very stiffly.*

LAWRENCE: Soldiers! A great lie is being whispered round India. The Government wants to interfere with your religion. Do you believe that? It's perfectly true that governments used to interfere with your religion. In the bad old days. Before the British came. Until a year ago when the province of Oudh came under British rule, no Hindu would have dared build a temple here in Lucknow. But all that's changed now. Throughout India Hindus and Mohammedans worship in peace. You can see it, you know it, you don't need me to tell you.

>*Pause.*

Search the world! You'll find no Government to compare with the British Government. In power, in wealth, in dominions. There is no sea on which the British Navy does not float. No clime where there are not British troops. And no other Government in the world cares for its soldiers as ours does. You can see it, you know it, you don't need me to tell you.

Pause.

We are assembled here today to reward three good and faithful soldiers. They caught people spreading lies and there are now fifty soldiers of the 7th Oudh Infantry locked up and awaiting their fate as mutineers. In a moment you will see the fine presents which we shall give to these three faithful men. But you are also here to be reminded that we are equally swift to punish. All powerful and irresistible, our Government will inflict such punishment as shall not easily pass away from the recollection of men. You will see it, you know it, you don't need me to tell you.

Pause.

Subahdar!

SUBAHDAR comes to attention, does about turn, marches out and returns with small folding table on which are various gifts. He places it beside LAWRENCE, then stands at attention beside it.

LAWRENCE: Now advance, Havildar and you two sepoys!

HAVILDAR and SEPOYS march in stiffly, salute and stand in front of the table.

Receive these magnificent gifts from the Government which is proud to call you its soldiers! Accept these honorary sabres! Take these sums of money for your families! Wear these robes of honour in your homes and at your festivals! May the splendid example you have set be followed – as most surely it will – in every regiment in the Army!

He hands out gifts, shakes hands with each recipient, then he and they stand to attention.

SUBAHDAR: Parade! 'Shun!

Sound of regiments coming to attention. LAWRENCE salutes. Triumphant bugle call. When it is over, LAWRENCE marches out, followed by the three recipients, followed by SUBAHDAR with the folding table.

Scene 32. *Tanganyika. 1858.*

Enter BURTON, JOHN HANNING SPEKE and SEEDY BOMBAY. BOMBAY, *an African ex-slave, a powerful, ugly man, supports* BURTON, *who can scarcely walk – his legs being paralysed by a severe attack of malaria – and leads* SPEKE, *who has a retinal infection and cannot see.* BURTON's *eyesight is also poor, since he is still recovering from the same infection.* SPEKE, *30, from an old family of the Somerset gentry, is a handsome, athletic man.*

BURTON: A streak of light! Down there! Straight through the trees. Is it?

SPEKE: Why ask me? I can't see the damned ground in front of my feet.

BURTON: A fine, useful pair of explorers we make! The lame leading the blind. Seedy Bombay, is that a streak of light? And if so, what is it?

BOMBAY: My opinion is, Captain Burton, that is the water.

BURTON: *The* water? The great lake the Arabs told us about? Lake Tanganyika?

BOMBAY: I think so.

BURTON: It's nothing but a creek. Great God! Have we ruined our health and looked death in the face to come out at some stinking backwater? Damn their lies! Curse their cheating souls to hell! I'm buggered if I'll go a step further.

He collapses on the ground. SPEKE *stands limply beside him.* BOMBAY *leaves them and goes on a little way.*

SPEKE: What's to be done?

BURTON: Nothing.

BOMBAY: *(shouting back)* Captain Burton!

BURTON: Go back and try the other lake.

SPEKE: I don't fancy that. If the Arabs exaggerated this one, they're probably wrong about Nyanza too. Unless you misunderstood what they said.

BURTON: I misunderstood?

SPEKE: Somebody did and I don't speak the lingo.

BURTON: Is that something to boast about? I'm beginning to wonder what you do have to boast about, Speke. You know no language but your own and a smattering of kitchen Hindustani. You haven't a shred of interest in the country or its people. You antagonise the porters.

SPEKE: Antagonise the porters! It's not possible to make those cretins more antagonistic than they naturally are. As for the country and its people, they're shit and if you weren't in such a foul temper you'd agree with me.

BURTON: I do agree with you.

BOMBAY: Captain Burton!

BURTON: But it's not enough to write them off as shit. It's crude, it's unhelpful, it doesn't advance the sum of human knowledge. In what does their shittiness consist?

SPEKE: Oh, for God's sake, it covers everything!

BURTON: Yes, but there are variations to be observed. The coastal tribes, for instance, are systematic liars. They tell lies where less clever men would tell the truth. The Wanyika, on the other hand, are utterly futile. Barbarians. Always drunk. Always fucking one another's wives. Always leaping about the place and breaking things. Always talking. Idle. Greedy. Cowardly. The Wagago are also idle and debauched. They spend their lives in one long coma of crapulence and drunkenness. They'd rather be beaten to death than descend to the level of their women and use a hoe. Only one thing makes them sit up and take an interest: thieving. They're expert thieves. Now cruelty, the pleasure in inflicting pain, is common to all these tribes. Their religious and social rites are foul and bloody, quite unlike those of the Hindu. It's not so much a lack of civilization as a case of arrested development. What's the explanation?

SPEKE: Look in the Bible! Noah blessed Shem and Japhet and cursed Ham. The Negro is an inferior race.

BURTON: What ignorance! What unspeakable humbug! Look at the climate! Look at the diseases! Look at us, two semi-corpses, two angry scarecrows! We've only been here a few months. What are we going to be like after years? What are our children going to be like? Have you noticed the negro children? They're lively, intelligent, physically superior to European children. Something happens to them at puberty. As if they could get no further, as if something in the blood suddenly incapacitated them. Diseases passed on by the parents. And the slave-trade! The best among them sold by the worst. What would centuries of that do to a people?

SPEKE: You stick to your explanation and I'll stick to mine. The result's the same. Apart from anything else, this is a shocking country for sport. Literally nothing but elephants. Plus a few antelopes and the odd guineafowl. I never had worse shooting. What a hell-hole!

BOMBAY: *(approaching)* Captain Burton, I help you up. You must go a bit farther.

BURTON struggles to his feet with BOMBAY's help.

BURTON: What have you found, Seedy Bombay? Something for Jack to shoot?

BOMBAY: Look there, please!

He leads BURTON on a little way, SPEKE stumbling behind.

BURTON: By God, it's the lake! We couldn't see it because of the trees. It's vast. An inland sea. Some great river must flow out of this. Why not the Nile? Congratulations, Jack! You and I are the first white men ever to set eyes on Lake Tanganyika.

SPEKE: I haven't set eyes on it.

BURTON: True. Bad luck, old man. I am the first. On Seedy! We've made it.

> *They go out.*

Scene 33. Cawnpore. 1857.

A hospital barracks inside the British entrenchment. A heavy fusillade off. Two exhausted, sweating NCOs – one British, one Indian – in tattered, dusty uniforms, are returning the fire from windows. On the floor lies a wounded man crying for water. Suddenly the outer door flies open and CAPTAIN MOORE darts in, bent double. He closes and bolts the door behind him.

MOORE: Got it! *(He waves a water-bottle)*

> The fusillade dies away and the two NCOs stop firing. MOORE kneels down and gives the bottle to the wounded man. Enter GENERAL SIR HUGH WHEELER, 68, with MAJOR MANNING.

WHEELER: Captain Moore, that was a foolhardy thing to do.

MOORE: Only way to get water, sir. They've got a beeline on the bit of open ground between here and the well.

WHEELER: We can't spare you. I'd rather fetch it myself.

MOORE: You'd never make it, sir.

HAVILDAR: *(at window)*: Look out! Get down!

> Crash of cannon off. All fling themselves down or move out of the way as a ball passes through the window and kills the wounded man on the floor. MANNING picks up the water-bottle and hands it to MOORE.

WHEELER: Those gunners are too damned accurate.

MOORE: We trained them ourselves, sir.

SERGEANT: *(at window)* They're coming over the trench! No, hold it! It's one man, with a white flag.

MOORE: It's a woman.

WHEELER: What is this, Moore? A trick?

MOORE: You know them better than I do, sir.

MANNING: Some sort of insult?

WHEELER: That may be, Major Manning.

INDIAN WOMAN: *(off)* General Wheeler? I have letter for General Wheeler.

WHEELER: Let her in. But for God's sake don't show yourself at the door.

MANNING: You're accepting the insult?

WHEELER: Don't be an ass, Manning. We're long past insults and we don't even know it is one.

> MOORE *opens door, admits* INDIAN WOMAN, *and bolts door behind her.*

MANNING: She's a half-caste.

WHEELER: Well, there's some subtlety in that.

INDIAN WOMAN: General Wheeler? Letter from Maharajah.

WHEELER: The Maharajah is dead. Some time ago.

INDIAN WOMAN: New Maharajah. Old Maharajah's heir.

WHEELER: You mean the Nana Sahib? His claim to the title was turned down.

INDIAN WOMAN: Nana Sahib is now Maharajah. He is ruling Cawnpore.

MOORE: Not yet he isn't. Not this bit of Cawnpore.

> WHEELER *has been reading letter and now passes it to* MANNING.

WHEELER: It's an invitation to surrender.

MANNING: Unacceptable.

MOORE: What are the terms?

WHEELER: We are to evacuate the position, leaving behind the guns and all but personal firearms. Safe conduct to the Ganges and boats to convey us to Allahabad.

MOORE: Sounds all right.

MANNING: Sounds all right? It's surrender, victory to the mutineers, after all we've been through.

WHEELER: Our position is pretty hopeless, Major Manning. We're outnumbered at least ten to one and losing men every day. We're burdened with women and children. Inadequate food, hardly any medical supplies or ammunition remaining, our only water-supply exposed to enemy fire. We've survived for three weeks, but how much longer?

MOORE: Nana offers us his personal safe-conduct.

MANNING: I'd trust that like a dose of strychnine.

MOORE: He was a good friend to us once, even if he is our bitter enemy now.

MANNING: Slimy bastard!

WHEELER: I don't think that's quite fair, Manning. My wife and I were frequently entertained by him in the old days. My wife, after all, is Indian herself and has some respect for him. Whatever the rights and wrongs, he was clumsily treated by the Government.

MOORE: He sent us advance warning of the sepoys' attack.

MANNING: And directed the attack himself.

WHEELER: Obviously he's an enemy. We've no reason to think him treacherous.

MANNING: If it's not treacherous to murder people you've entertained in your own house, the world's turned upside down.

MOORE: We can hold out for a few days more, but there's no hope of being relieved in that time. What good will it do him to butcher eight hundred defenceless people? He's got what he came for, his title, his power and the expulsion of the British.

WHEELER: In your opnion, Moore, we should accept this offer?

MOORE: If we want to survive.

WHEELER: After fifty-three years' service with the Indian, I thought I understood him. This past month I've lost my way. *(to INDIAN WOMAN)* Tell the Nana Sahib that we accept these terms.

MOORE opens door and lets INDIAN WOMAN out.

MANNING: I don't give a nag's fart for our chances.

WHEELER: I never did, but we've done pretty well all the same. Enough's enough.

He goes out.

MANNING: It's clear Wheeler's lost his nerve. Have you?

MOORE: I don't fancy going out to the well again. *(He empties bottle and throws it down)* Do you?

MANNING goes out.

MOORE: *(to SERGEANT and HAVILDAR)* Give me a hand with Williams!

They carry out the dead man.

Scene 34. Tanganyika. 1858.

Early morning. BURTON in his tent, writing a letter.

BURTON: 'Dearest Isabel, we haven't found the Nile. We sailed across Lake Tanganyika, but only found a river that flowed in, none that flowed out. Speke's gone off to look at another lake mentioned by the Arabs. I felt too weak and stayed behind to write up my notes. I daresay he's really gone to kill a few animals and eat their embryos. I doubt if I could face another expedition with him. The British character personified, brave and true, but obstinate, shallow, conventional and self-satisfied.

Distant shouts.

Experience, instead of broadening his mind seems to reveal it as a narrower and narrower channel . . .'

Enter SEEDY BOMBAY.

BOMBAY: Captain Burton, we're returned.

BURTON: Seedy Bombay!

They embrace.

You found the lake?

BOMBAY: We found it. Very, very big.

BURTON: Bravo! And Captain Speke is well?

BOMBAY: Quite well, sir. He's here.

Enter SPEKE.

BURTON: Jack!

SPEKE: Richard!

They shake hands.

BURTON: Worth the excursion?

SPEKE: Very much so!

BURTON: Shoot anything?

SPEKE: Couple of red geese. By way of celebration. They were on the lake, which I've called Victoria Nyanza.

BURTON: Currying Royal favour?

SPEKE: It seemed appropriate.

BURTON: Half Africa will be called Victoria by the time the British have finished with it. What about some breakfast?

SPEKE: By George, yes! Breakfast, Seedy!

BOMBAY: Are you talking to me, Captain Speke, or to some houseboy?

He goes out.

SPEKE: I'm sorry you didn't come, Richard, because I've found it.

BURTON: Found what?

SPEKE: Victoria Nyanza is the source of the Nile.

BURTON: You're joking.

SPEKE: I mean it.

BURTON: There was a notice to say so?

SPEKE: It's the logical deduction. The lake must be the largest in Africa. It stretches so far north that no one knows its length and it's so broad you can't see the other side. If the Mountains of the Moon rise from its western shore, then some great river must drain out from the north. What river can that be but the Nile? I tell you, I stood for the first time on the southern shore of that great lake and all my doubts left me. I knew it was the source of the Nile.

BURTON: You knew it was the source of the Nile, so it must be the source of the Nile? That's the way women argue.

SPEKE: You don't accept what I say?

BURTON: I don't accept your argument, Jack. I accept your great moment of inspiration, of course. Your Excalibur dream on the banks of the lake.

SPEKE: What you mean is, you don't want it to be the source of the Nile.

BURTON: I mean that you very much want it to be. Unfortunately you haven't enough evidence to convince a child of ten, let alone a serious geographer. Now give me your observations, what you actually saw, and I'll write them up in my notes . . .

SPEKE: Will you come back with me and see the lake for yourself?

BURTON: What good would that be? We need proof. We're both tired, it's a hell of a long way back to the sea still and we haven't the resources left for more exploration. Therefore we return to England, fit out another expedition and come back. That's the sensible and scientific thing to do. Our feminine intuitions are best kept to ourselves. Agreed?

SPEKE: I'll say nothing more about it.

BURTON: That's the spirit. Now if we want any breakfast we'd better go and smooth down Seedy Bombay. He may look black to you, but to me he looks like the backbone of this expedition.

They go out.

Scene 35. *Cawnpore. 1857.*

A wooden bridge over the Ganges. Enter NANA SAHIB and AZIMULLA.

AZIMULLA: There they go, Maharajah. See how thin and weary they are now, those once proud sahibs. Look at those haughty memsahibs sitting in the bullock carts with their starving children! Human refuse! Down they go to the Ganges and the boats will take their stink out of our noses. And so down the river to the sea. The refuse leaving Cawnpore joins all the other refuse being swept out of India.

NANA: Why so vengeful, Azimulla? Do you want to kick people when they are down?

AZIMULLA: What other time to kick them?

NANA: More subtle not to.

AZIMULLA: I don't understand that.

NANA: No, but the British do. Look, if I say to you, I am going to kick you because you are down, that is physical humiliation.

AZIMULLA: Very painful.

NANA: But now if I say to you. I am *not* going to kick you because you are down, that is moral humiliation. More painful.

AZIMULLA: The British have taught us something.

NANA: How to be always on top, that is what they've taught us.

AZIMULLA: They're at the bottom now.

NANA: It is not so simple as to drive them out of Cawnpore, or even out of India.

AZIMULLA: Victory is to the strongest.

NANA: But how do you judge which is strongest?

AZIMULLA: They have surrendered to us.

NANA: So few of them, so many of us. They have preserved their women and children, they are still carrying arms. They have behaved well.

Enter TANTIA TOPI.

TOPI: Everything ready, Maharajah. The British are just going on board the boats.

NANA: And the sepoys?

TOPI: Also ready. One thousand sepoys concealed along the banks of the river, with cannons and a detachment of cavalry.

NANA: The signal?

TOPI: I wave my hand from this bridge. A bugler is watching. The bugle-call is the signal.

NANA: Wise precautions!

AZIMULLA: What do you mean to do, Maharajah?

NANA: I am still considering.

TOPI: The sepoys are murmuring. They think it dishonourable to break the treaty.

NANA: What do they know about it? Am I going to break the treaty? On the other hand, if it is my purpose to destroy an enemy, what do I care about treaties?

AZIMULLA: It would give moral superiority to the British.

NANA: You think so, Azimulla? Well, let us consider. Suppose I let them go safely down the river. I behave well, by their standards. However, they have also behaved well. Perhaps they have behaved better, seeing they are so few. Who is the winner? Now suppose them all dead. Can they be the winners? Am I not in any case the loser if I behave according to their ideas of what is moral and honourable?

AZIMULLA: The boats are almost ready to leave.

TOPI: Maharajah, you must not only consider your own feelings – understandable when you think how the British have treated you in the past – but also the feelings of your soldiers.

NANA: Why is that, Tantia Topi?

TOPI: They chose you as their leader. They wish to drive out the British. But they don't hate the British. It was a strange sight, the British coming out of their entrenchment. Our sepoys broke ranks and ran to meet them. They shook hands with their old officers. They helped the women into the carts and carried the children. They all laughed and discussed the siege together, the sepoys telling the British that never in all their days had they heard of such a brave defence by so few against so many.

NANA: What do you mean by telling me this?

TOPI: I mean to show you the respect which the sepoys still feel for their enemies.

NANA: Go and look over the bridge!

TOPI does so.

Are all the British embarked?

TOPI: Nearly all. They are just casting off the first boat.

NANA: Raise your arm!

TOPI: Maharajah! It's not wise.

NANA: Wave your arm, Tantia Topi, or you'll be hanged from this bridge.

TOPI waves his arm. A bugle-call sounds, followed

immediately by volleys of rifle-fire, cannon-fire and screaming.

AZIMULLA: I don't understand why you've done this, Maharajah.

NANA: A great rage came over me. I'm tired of moral contortions. I am the stronger. Why shouldn't I use my strength?

He goes out.

TOPI: What is he talking about? This was weakness, not strength.

He and AZIMULLA go out.

Scene 36. Tasmania. 1858.

Enter BONWICK, *a journalist*, and DANDRIDGE, *Superintendent of the Aborigines. Wind and rain. Door or shutter banging regularly.*

BONWICK: Phew! This is a cheerless spot. Are you Mr. Dandridge?

DANDRIDGE: Right.

BONWICK: Superintendent of the Aborigines?

DANDRIDGE: Right.

BONWICK: I'm from The Hobart Town Gazette. Name's Bonwick. There's been a letter written to our paper, Mr. Dandridge, about the condition of the aborigines.

DANDRIDGE: Oh yes?

BONWICK: How many remain in your care?

DANDRIDGE: Dozen or so. Don't count them every day.

BONWICK: You mean you may have lost one or two since you last counted them?

DANDRIDGE: They're not too healthy.

BONWICK: Do you wonder? Apart from being the back of bloody beyond, this place is a slum.

DANDRIDGE: Doesn't appeal to me.

BONWICK: Windows all broken. Door hanging off its hinges. Roof leaking. Not even a stick of furniture.

DANDRIDGE: Not my idea of a cosy home. I live in Hobart.

BONWICK: These people are costing the government two thousand a year.

DANDRIDGE: Right.

BONWICK: Where do they sleep?

DANDRIDGE: Some of them sleep in here.

BONWICK: And the others?

DANDRIDGE: The women sleep with the timber-workers.

BONWICK: Don't they have blankets, the ones that sleep here?

DANDRIDGE: They did have.

BONWICK: Where are they now?

BONWICK: Most likely sold to the timber-workers. They sell everything they don't smash.

BONWICK: What do they do with the money?

DANDRIDGE: They don't sell for money. For liquor.

BONWICK: Don't they have anything to occupy them? Cultivation? Handicrafts?

DANDRIDGE: That's the garden. It used to be cultivated in Mr. Clark's day, until his wife died. Then he lost heart and died soon afterwards himself. Not a healthy spot, this.

BONWICK: Shouldn't some effort be made to improve it?

DANDRIDGE: How do you mean?

BONWICK: Repair the buildings. Clear the garden. Teach the aborigines to take more pride in themselves and their surroundings.

DANDRIDGE: It's been tried. They just slip back to their old ways. Why not? It's their life, they don't reckon with ours.

BONWICK: I suppose you still give them Christian instruction.

DANDRIDGE: They never were Christians, never will be. I don't like people interfering with my life, no more do they.

They're not children, are they? Matter of fact, they're all fairly long in the tooth.

BONWICK: You feel no pity for them? Abandoned like this to a slow, miserable extinction.

DANDRIDGE: They get their rations from the government. Tea, sugar, meat, flour, I dole them out every week. They had furniture and blankets till they flogged them. You might say they've abandoned themselves. Yes, they're pitiful creatures.

They go out.

Scene 37. Cawnpore. 1857.

NANA SAHIB *is seated on cushions, smoking a nargileh, with food and drink beside him, watching a girl dance. Near him stands* TANTIA TOPI. *Musicians play off-stage.*

TOPI: Royal Highness, it's not yet time to take our ease. The British relief force is advancing from Allahabad.

NANA: Rather a scratch team. Hastily assembled, not many guns, no cavalry. Not a serious threat. Our troops will smash them.

TOPI: Nevertheless, you should either release those prisoners or kill them. As long as you keep them here the British will think of nothing but recapturing Cawnpore.

NANA: I am not afraid of the British. How do you like this dancer, Tantia Topi?

TOPI: Royal Highness, it's not civilized to confine two hundred women and children in a house built for one person.

NANA: No, but good for these former memsahibs. To find themselves in a little pleasure-house built by a white sahib for his native mistress. They are grinding corn for me. When their discomfort and menial tasks have made a sufficient effect on them, I may perhaps release a few. As an example.

TOPI: Of what? Indian brutality?

NANA: Humility. I sent Azimulla to London in the days of British pride, to ask the Company Directors for my rights as heir to the Maharajah. They treated him, my representative, like a schoolboy asking for too many sweets. These people must either learn humility or perish. I shall be a missionary to the British.

Sound of hurried steps. The music stops abruptly. Enter AZIMULLA *in haste.*

AZIMULLA: Maharajah!

NANA: Azimulla, you've interrupted the dance.

AZIMULLA: The battle is lost. The British will be in Cawnpore tomorrow.

The dancer runs out.

NANA: Respect! Respect! You're all lacking in respect.

TOPI: We're doomed men.

AZIMULLA: Not as bad as that. They've no cavalry. We can join the Moulvie's army at Lucknow. But we must hurry.

TOPI: If it wasn't for the massacre on the river, if it wasn't for the prisoners, they'd have left Cawnpore alone.

NANA: Tantia Topi, find some sepoys! Take them to the Beebeegurh and order them to shoot through the windows. No woman or child is to live. Go and do it!

TOPI goes out.

That man is weak.

AZIMULLA: It's not a strong action to shoot the prisoners.

NANA: Why not?

AZIMULLA: It will look like panic. The British force is small and exhausted. True, they can enter Cawnpore, but our army can regroup and enter the city in a few days.

NANA: Yes, but we can't take the prisoners with us.

AZIMULLA: Then leave them behind. These prisoners are a burden to us. We should not eliminate the burden, but pass it on to the British.

NANA: I like that. Go down and stop the killing.
Sound of shots

Nothing goes right. What is the matter? Am I an unlucky

man? Why did Lord Dalhousie refuse my petition to be the Maharajah's heir? Do I care who rules India? It was enough for me to be a prince and to receive the homage due to me. Battles! Killing! They are not in my nature.

Enter TANTIA TOPI.

TOPI: Royal Highness, the sepoys . . .

AZIMULLA: We heard the shooting.

TOPI: When they saw the women and children inside, they lost their nerve. They fired into the ceiling.

AZIMULLA: The prisoners are still alive?

TOPI: All alive. What now, Maharajah?

NANA: You tell me the sepoys have mutinied and you ask what now? Did they know the orders came from me?

TOPI: They knew.

NANA: Then I'll tell you what now. Go outside and have yourself shot!

AZIMULLA: But this is good news.

NANA: All useless. What can we do if we cannot rely on our own soldiers? They still admire the British. They bow to their moral superiority.

TOPI: They only felt compunction for defenceless people.

NANA: Would they have felt compunction if a British officer had ordered them to shoot prisoners? They would have obeyed like well-trained dogs. These dogs must be taught to turn on their masters. They must see their masters as only dogs like themselves. Yes, rabid dogs. I will make the British mad. Once and for all I will strip them of their moral superiority. Azimulla! I shall give you instructions. I want no more advice. No more arguments. My mind is now quite clear.

He goes out with AZIMULLA, speaking into his ear. TOPI follows at a distance.

Scene 38. Tanganyika. 1858.

The interior of a small, dark hut. SPEKE is heard screaming, then barking like a dog. BURTON is kneeling beside his bed. SEEDY BOMBAY standing nearby.

BURTON: Jack? Can you hear me?

SPEKE: A net made of hooks. Fastened into my flesh. They were dragging me. Faster and faster. Over the plain. Through thorn-bushes. Wild animals dragging me behind them.

BURTON: The natives say you've got the 'little irons'. Some sort of fever. You had a fit.

SPEKE: Richard, are you there?

BURTON: Still here beside you. *(Pause)* He's asleep. Bring some cold water and a cloth, Seedy.

BOMBAY goes out. After a few moments SPEKE begins to move about feverishly and then to mutter.

SPEKE: The bastard!

BURTON: Jack? What is it? Pain coming back?

SPEKE: His notes, always his. My observations go into his notes. He did it in Somaliland. Wants to do it with Victoria Nyanza. Knows very well I've discovered the Nile. Daren't admit it. Wants to make it his discovery.

BURTON: Jack, I can hear what you're saying.

Re-enter BOMBAY

SPEKE: Lies on his back all day, picking other people's brains. Writing up their discoveries as his. Swindler! Cheat! Thief!

BOMBAY: This is very bad sickness. Africans die.

SPEKE: Who'd trust him? His reputation. What he did in the

Karachi Brothels. Wallows in filth. An evil man. Does he set up to be the great explorer? The master? Because of his age and experience? What experience? Experience of boys' arseholes and women's cunts! Fuck your experience, Burton! Get out of my light!

BOMBAY: It is the devil speaking, not him.

BURTON: He means it.

BOMBAY: Captain Burton, you are a good man, especially to him. The devil always speaks opposite of what is true.

BURTON: I'm afraid this is the truth. As he sees it.

BOMBAY: Africa is full of devils. I am going to fetch witch-doctor. He can drive away devils. He knows them all like friends.

BOMBAY goes out. SPEKE starts to scream and writhe, banging his heels on the floor, turning his body from side to side. BURTON kneels beside him and forces the cloth between his teeth, fighting with him and holding him down. At last SPEKE grows calmer and opens his eyes.

SPEKE: They were cutting me up. Tearing out my sinews. Men with heads of lions.

BURTON: You're dreaming, Jack. They shan't have you.

SPEKE: Richard?

BURTON: I'm here. There's my hand.

SPEKE: The pain's gone. The knives are sheathed.

BURTON: Good for you!

He wipes SPEKE's face with the cloth.

Scene 39. Cawnpore. 1857.

Outside the Beebeegurh. Enter small detachment of soldiers marching in step, with SERGEANT *and* SUBALTERN.

SERGEANT: Squad, halt! There we are, sir. That must be it. The Beebeegurh.

SUBALTERN: It's tiny. You couldn't keep two hundred people in that.

SERGEANT: Not a soul here now. Corporal Tanner!

TANNER: Sergeant!

SERGEANT: Double round the back! Check the yard!

TANNER goes out. SUBALTERN goes and looks through doorway of house.

SUBALTERN: The house is quite empty. *(he suddenly leans against doorpost)* Sergeant!

SERGEANT: Sir! What's the matter, sir?

SUBALTERN: Look at the walls, Sergeant.

SERGEANT steps past him into doorway.

SERGEANT: Christ Almighty!

SUBALTERN: Isn't it blood?

SERGEANT: Not just the walls, sir.

He backs out of doorway and stands there looking at his feet. Blood covers his boots.

It's the whole floor. Two feet deep.

SUBALTERN: My God!

SERGEANT: Put your head between your knees, sir. Right down.

SUBALTERN moves aside to be sick.

SERGEANT: Evans!

EVANS: Sergeant!

SERGEANT: Go and find me a native. Drag him out of his house if you have to, but bring him to me at the double!

EVANS goes out.

SUBALTERN: I'm sorry.

SERGEANT: You're straight out from England, sir.

SUBALTERN: I didn't mind the fighting.

SERGEANT: Best not look at my boots, sir.

Enter TANNER.

TANNER: Round in the yard! There's a well.

SERGEANT: What about it?

TANNER: I didn't look too closely.

SERGEANT: Show me!

SERGEANT and TANNER go out hurriedly.
SUBALTERN sits with his back against wall of house.

RAMAYAN SULIN: *(off)* I know very well that this is called Beebeeburh. It was built by Englishmen. I know nothing else about it.

Enter SULIN, shepherded by EVANS.

EVANS: *(saluting SUBALTERN)* Prisoner, sir! Hiding in a doorway.

SULIN: I was not hiding. About to insert key. Door of my own home.

SUBALTERN: Something has happened here. What do you know about it?

SULIN: Nothing at all. I am respectable citizen of Cawnpore. Ramayan Sulin, well-known lawyer practising in this city.

SUBALTERN: Did you know that there were two hundred British women and children shut up in this small house?

SULIN: How should I know that? Am I in the Nana Sahib's confidence? I am not even supporter of the Nana. Personally I welcome return of British. This rebellion, sir, is not connected with civilian population, purely military.

Enter SERGEANT and TANNER.

SERGEANT: The bodies are in the well, sir. It's stuffed to the top. Who's this?

SUBALTERN: He's not very helpful.

SERGEANT: Not very helpful? We'll see about that.

SULIN: I assure you I am quite ignorant. I would strongly advise you to look for somebody else better informed.

SERGEANT: Don't give me that fucking claptrap! You were in Cawnpore, you know what happened, first and last.

SULIN: Of course we heard that the Nana had taken prisoners after the massacre, but whether all were in this house... I was not visiting this part of the city myself...

SERGEANT hits him in the face.

SERGEANT: Think again, you black bastard!

SUBALTERN: Go easy, Sergeant. No call for violence.

SERGEANT: No call for violence? If you've stopped throwing up, sir, perhaps you'd go and take a look at that well and then tell me if there's no call for violence.

SUBALTERN: Mr. Sulin, were you aware of what's in the well?

SULIN: Not at all.

SERGEANT: Come on! *(threatening to strike him again)*

SULIN: Let me say that of course there were rumours flying about the city, but as a lawyer I am accustomed always to seek evidence at first hand and not to trust rumours.

SERGEANT: Just you come with me, then! *(pulls him to doorway of house)* Now look in there! Is that floor evidence at first hand or is it a bloody mirage?

SULIN: Horrifying sight!

SERGEANT: You were in Cawnpore and you knew nothing about it?

SULIN: I am hearing rumours? Not liking to believe them. Not having opportunity to check them myself.

SERGEANT: Then you can check them now.

He pushes SULIN down inside the doorway.

SUBALTERN: Sergeant!

SERGEANT: Sir!

SUBALTERN: Please leave this to me.

SERGEANT: No, sir, you leave it to me. I'm going to have the truth out of this bugger if I lose my stripes for it. Keep out of my way, sir! Nobody thinks much of an officer who gets hit by his own men. He doesn't make it, sir. Take my advice!

SULIN, smeared with blood, is getting up.

Now you speak up or you're going to get hurt!

SULIN: I'm not clear exactly what you're wanting.

SERGEANT: Evans! Jackson! Hold his man while I tell him what

I'm wanting.

After covert glances at SUBALTERN, chewing his lip to one side, EVANS and JACKSON take hold of SULIN.

Now you, get this straight. Nothing and nobody is going to come between you and me. First question: who did this?

SULIN: Without a shadow of doubt, the Nana Sahib.

SERGEANT: With his own hands?

SULIN: He must be employing assassins.

SERGEANT: Come on, you can do better than that!

SULIN: Rumour is speaking of five men.

SERGEANT: Five men killed two hundred people?

SULIN: With knives. Long knives. It is act of savagery. No person in Cawnpore is approving this act. Guilty persons have left the city. Only innocent persons remaining behind to receive British.

SERGEANT: Not one man of you is innocent. You're all savages. Throw him down!

EVANS and JACKSON hesitate, looking at SUBALTERN. SERGEANT punches SULIN in stomach.

I said, throw him down.

They do so.

Now push his face in it!

SULIN struggles violently.

Go on! Right in it!

They are doing so, when the SUBALTERN suddenly glances

off stage and springs to attention.

SUBALTERN: Colonel Neill! On your feet!

SERGEANT: Squad, fall in! 'Shun!

All but SULIN get into some sort of line and come to attention. SULIN remains lying where he is, his face coated in blood. Enter COLONEL NEILL, 47, a Scot from a military family. SUBALTERN salutes. NEILL returns salute. Silence, while he takes in the man on the ground, the condition he's in and the state of SERGEANT's boots.

NEILL: There's been a crime?

SUBALTERN: It's so horrible, sir, what we've found, that I'm afraid we lost control of ourselves.

NEILL: The prisoners have been murdered?

SERGEANT: Cut up, sir. Like butcher's meat. Crammed into the well behind the house, sir. Women and children, sir, legs and arms and pieces of skin and bone. We found this man lurking nearby, sir. He pretended to know nothing. We questioned him . . .

SULIN: I am appealing for redress, Colonel Sahib. I am completely innocent. Never did I think British could behave like barbarians.

NEILL: You call *us* barbarians? What did you do to him, Sergeant? Why is his face covered in blood?

SERGEANT: Not his blood, sir. I may have gone too far, sir, feeling as I did, in the heat of the moment. I would just ask you, sir, to look inside this house.

NEILL walks to doorway and looks inside for some moments, then he returns to the others.

NEILL: Ensign!

SUBALTERN: Sir!

NEILL: You are to erect a gallows beside this house. At fourteen hundred hours I shall sit in judgment on this suspect. If I find him guilty of supporting the mutiny, he is to be brought here and compelled to clean the floor with his tongue. If necessary the lash is to be used until he does so. Immediately afterwards he is to be hanged. In the same manner we shall treat every person in Cawnpore who can be shown to be implicated in this deed, until every stain of blood has been removed from this house. Let the treatment of the guilty men be as revolting to their feelings as possible. By these means we shall demonstrate to all Indians and to all peoples throughout the world, now and in the time to come, that such a deed is beyond the pale of humanity.

He turns and goes out. SUBALTERN salutes.

SERGEANT: Bring the prisoner, then!

The soldiers seize SULIN.

Quick march!

They go out, the SUBALTERN following.

Scene 40. Kew Gardens. 1859.

ISABEL and BURTON enter.

ISABEL: The last thing he said to you?

BURTON: The very last thing as we shook hands in Aden. 'Trust me! I won't go near the Royal Geographical Society. Not until you turn up and we can go there together.'

ISABEL: Why did you let him come home before you?

BURTON: Why not? A ship called in with a spare berth. Speke was fed up with Aden, I still didn't feel up to the voyage, so he took it.

ISABEL: You had no suspicion?

BURTON: If I had, I must have squashed it. Weakness? Indolence? Or maybe a sort of final test. As if I'd said to myself; This man and I have been through Hell together. We've seen and suffered the worst this world is capable of and we've survived. I saved his life. If I can't trust him, what's left?

ISABEL: He must have felt the same himself or he wouldn't have said so deliberately, 'Trust me!'

BURTON: The day after he reaches England he goes straight to the Royal Geographical Society and tells Murchison that he's discovered the source of the Nile. Not just that. That he was the real leader of the expedition. That without him I'd never have made the journey. That I was more interested in the sexual customs of the natives than in geographical discovery. That I denied his great achievement and refused to go near Nyanza. That I had to be coaxed and carried back to the coast. That finally I lay on my back in Aden because I was afraid to come home with him and admit my inferiority.

ISABEL: It's unbelievable.

BURTON: I thought I knew the man. Even when he was delirious and poured out his hatred for me, I didn't take it entirely seriously. Those long evenings in the tent, we used to read together – Shakespeare, Euclid, anything I'd brought with me – it was all new to him. How to observe scientifically, how to write up his notes. Each day he'd bring me what he'd done for correction. How to sketch the scenery. It's like the Arab tag:

'I taught him archery, yes, all I knew,
'and when his arm grew strong, 'twas me he slew.'

ISABEL: But you say Lake Nyanza is not the source of the Nile.

BURTON: I'm nearly sure it's not and he's got no proof that it is. I'd place a fairly large bet on my lake, Tanganyika.

ISABEL: Then he's gained nothing but a little temporary notoriety. You must go back to Africa and prove him wrong.

BURTON: You underrate the man. What he's gained from the Royal Geographical Society is another expedition. Which he's to lead and from which I'm excluded. When I asked to be allowed to lead a second expedition, starting from a different point, I was more or less told to leave the building. He's utterly destroyed my reputation. I'm a pariah.

ISABEL: People are not such fools.

BURTON: *(laying his head on her knee)* Isabel, I'm ready to despair. I've been robbed of the last important thing I could have done with my life.

ISABEL: *(stroking his head)* My darling, my darling! It's not true. You are the person you are. He can't take that away from you. Let him have his stolen day of triumph! When you've got your health back you'll feel differently. History will decide between you. I know who you are. I love you and admire you more than anyone else on earth. Isn't there any meaning in that?

Scene 41. Trieste. 1884.

OLD BURTON and ISABEL *are in the garden of their house. He is seated in a deck-chair, she at a garden table, taking dictation.*

OLD BURTON: 'Then Nur-al-Din lapsed into a swoon, the forerunner of death; but presently recovering himself he said, "O Hasan, O my son, I will now bequeth to thee five last behests. The First Behest is, Be overintimate with none, nor frequent any, nor be familiar with any; so shalt thou be safe from his mischief . . ."'

OLD ISABEL: How typically Arab!

OLD BURTON: Yes, I shall add a footnote: 'Quite true! Very unadvisable to dive below the surface of one's acquaintances, but such intimacy is like marriage of which Johnson said, "Without it there is no pleasure in life."'

OLD ISABEL: I wonder what you mean by that.

OLD BURTON: Isn't it clear?

OLD ISABEL: You think being married has done you mischief?

OLD BURTON: 'Without it there is no pleasure in life.'

OLD ISABEL: But mischief too.

OLD BURTON: I was mainly thinking of Speke. Why did he do that to me?

OLD ISABEL: He was put up to it by that man he met on the boat home from Aden. Laurence Oliphant.

OLD BURTON: Jack must have really wanted to do it, all the same.

OLD ISABEL: He regretted it afterwards.

OLD BURTON: You think so?

OLD ISABEL: I know so. He wanted to make it up with you that dreadful day at Bath, the British Association meeting when you were to argue against one another, with Livingstone as referee. But you gave him a cold stare and he was afraid of you. Then he went out and shot himself.

OLD BURTON: It was an accident.

OLD ISABEL: Was it?

OLD BURTON: Probably not. An accident on purpose. When all the time he was right and I was wrong about the Nile. Poor Jack! So he died young and twenty years later I live on, just, still in the shadow of his treacherous, unnecessary slander. How appalling history is, always with the worst ending! How much better the stories we tell ourselves, that come right at last, on the thousand and first night!

He picks up his manuscript and goes on dictating.

'"The Second Behest is, O my son: Deal harshly with none lest fortune with thee deal hardly; for the fortune of this world is one day with thee and another day against thee and all worldly goods are but a loan to be repaid."'

OTHER PLAYS AND FILMSCRIPTS FROM THE SAME PUBLISHERS

Marco Bellocchio
CHINA IS NEAR

Ingmar Bergman
FACE TO FACE
A FILM TRILOGY (Through a Glass Darkly, The Communicants, The Silence)
PERSONA AND SHAME
SCENES FROM A MARRIAGE
THE SERPENT'S EGG
TWO SCREENPLAYS (Blood of a Poet, Testament of Orpheus)

Gabriel Cousin
BLACK OPERA & THE GIRL WHO BARKS LIKE A DOG

Witold Gombrowicz
THE MARRIAGE
OPERETTA
PRINCESS IVONA

Kaj Hummelstrup
WELCOME TO DALLAS, MR. KENNEDY

Alexandro Jodorowsky
EL TOPO

Leroi Jones
FOUR BLACK REVOLUTIONARY PLAYS (Experimental Death Unit 1, A Black Mass, Great Goodness of Life and Madheart)

Kenneth Jupp
A CHELSEA TRILOGY

Charles Marowitz
ARTAUD AT RODEZ
THE MAROWITZ SHAKESPEARE (Hamlet, Macbeth, The Shrew, Measure for Measure, The Merchant of Venice)
SEX WARS
THE SHREW

Mustapha Matura
AS TIME GOES BY & BLACK PIECES

Robert Nye
PENTHESILEA, FUGUE & SISTERS

Robert Nye & Bill Watson
SAWNEY BEAN

Peter Redgrove
MISS CARSTAIRS DRESSED FOR BLOODING, THREE PIECES FOR VOICES & IN THE COUNTRY OF THE SKIN

Paul Ritchie
SAINT HONEY & OH DAVID ARE YOU THERE?

Tadeusz Rozewicz
THE CARD INDEX (The Interupted Act & Gone Out)
THE WITNESSES (The Funny Man & The Old Woman Broods)

Jeremy Sandford
CATHY COME HOME
EDNA THE INEBRIATE WOMAN
SMILING DAVID

Anthony Shaffer
MURDERER
SLEUTH

Yevgeny Shvarts
THE NAKED KING (The Shadow & The Dragon)

John Spurling
IN THE HEART OF THE BRITISH MUSEUM
MACRUNE'S GUEVARA
SHADES OF HEATHCLIFF & DEATH OF CAPTAIN DOUGHTY

Martin Walser
THE RABBIT RACE & THE DETOUR

Peter Weiss
DISCOURSE ON VIETNAM
THE INVESTIGATION
THE MARAT/SADE

Edgar White
LAMENT FOR RASTAFARI & LIKE THEM THAT DREAM

Naftali Yavin
PRECIOUS MOMENTS